WOMEN & PASSION

M. Sara Rosenthal

Prentice Hall Canada

A Pearson Company

Toronto

For Tanya, who touched my life when she felt hers.

Canadian Cataloguing in Publication Data

Rosenthal, M. Sara
    Women & passion

ISBN 0-13-088404-9

1. Women – Sexual behavior. 2. Sex (Psychology). 3. Women – Psychology.
4. Self-actualization (Psychology). I. Title. II. Title: Women and passion.

HQ1206.R27 2000   155.6'13   C00-931470-9

ISBN 0-13-088404-9

Editorial Director, Trade Division: Andrea Crozier
Acquisitions Editor: Nicole de Montbrun
Copy Editor: Liba Berry
Production Editor: Jodi Lewchuk
Art Direction: Mary Opper
Cover and Interior Design: Tania Craan
Cover Image: Masatomo Kuriya / Photonica
Author Photograph: Greg Edwards
Production Manager: Kathrine Pummell
Page Layout: Dave McKay

1 2 3 4 5 W 04 03 02 01 00

Printed and bound in Canada.

Visit our Web site! Send us your comments, browse our catalogues, and more.
www.phcanada.com.

A Pearson Company

CONTENTS

ACKNOWLEDGMENTS

First and foremost, I acknowledge that I am lucky to live in a part of the world where I can express my opinions on this subject. I am privileged to even ponder the subject of passion, because I have enough to eat, a roof over my head and a warm place to sleep.

Second, this book is made up of many voices other than my own, and I gratefully acknowledge the women interviewed for this book; I am honoured that they have allowed *Women & Passion* to be the conduit for their voices and stories.

Nicole de Montbrun, my editor at Prentice Hall Canada, championed and supported this project from day one. I thank her for allowing me the latitude to explore a topic so close to my heart and soul.

I was blessed with one of the most wonderful, passionate, not to mention beautiful, souls to grace this earth, my researcher and editorial everywoman. Larissa Kostoff breathed so much life into this project, it would not be what it is without her. When Larissa and I first discussed the project, we set out pouring over biographies of women, looking for patterns in passion. Then, long passionate discussions in Starbucks followed, which became springboards for much of the book's content. Larissa's gift in finding just the right quotes and sources inspired me throughout the crafting of this book. And she tirelessly listened to draft passages being read aloud, inserting valuable comments all the while.

Liba Berry, my copy editor, always meticulous, provided instrumental feedback and suggestions.

My mother listened endlessly to passages from this book, too. I knew I was on to something when she actually told me to "keep reading; this is interesting."

I also want to acknowledge the men in my life—both past and present—who were aware of the level of self-disclosure in this book. Their support helped me to be a little more courageous than I might have otherwise been.

Helen Lenskyi, Ph.D., Department of Sociology and Equity Studies, Ontario Institute for Studies in Education, University of Toronto, and Laura M. Purdy, Ph.D., Department of Philosophy, University of Toronto, and Bioethicist, University of Toronto Joint Centre for Bioethics, have been central figures in my understanding the complexities of feminist perspectives, a necessary skill when looking at women and passion.

I also wish to thank my medical advisors on a former book, *Women and Sadness*, which helped to lay some of the groundwork for this book: Debra Lander, M.D., F.R.C.P.C, Assistant Professor of Psychiatry, University of Manitoba; Mark Lander, M.D., F.R.C.P.C., Associate Professor of Psychiatry, University of Manitoba, and a member of the Mood Disorders Clinic, Health Sciences Centre, Winnipeg, Manitoba, and Sheila Lander, L.P.N./R.N., a psychiatric nurse practitioner, Health Sciences Centre, Winnipeg, Manitoba; and Judith Ross, Ph.D., Clinical Psychologist and Special Lecturer, Department of Psychology, University of Toronto. Other experts, ranging from social workers and counsellors, to feminist therapists, who gave me dozens of hours of their time and expertise for *Women and Sadness*, helped with the foundation of *Women & Passion*.

FOREWORD

Women & Passion couldn't be more timely. More and more, we celebrate the dynamic, confident "new" woman interested in power, money and sex. Women, whose lives are in transition, are taking a long, hard look at their needs, their desires, their hopes and their place in society. Where, they wonder, does an emotion such as passion fit into their new lifestyle?

There are women who have come to the conclusion that the best way to plough through the minefield of life is to suppress emotion. (Perhaps they've decided this is how men have managed to dominate and succeed throughout history!) Yet it is emotion that defines us as human beings, stimulating and propelling us to reach beyond the mundane and expand beyond our designated horizons.

And the most powerful emotion of all, no matter where it is encountered and no matter what makes it erupt, is passion. Passion is the driving force behind human survival, and nourishment of the soul for both men and women. It makes our existence fascinating, infuriating, joyful, agonizing and wholly worthwhile.

Those who know me might say my life—one spent succumbing to passion, especially of the sexual kind—has meant a life misspent in turmoil. I would argue that, while a life lived wildly and recklessly by most people's standards, it was and still is a life lived to the full.

There's always an assumption that my passion is narrowly focussed. (It isn't: there are many other areas of life for which I express passion.) The word passion, as mentioned in this fascinating book, has become almost exclusively associated with sexual fervour. Thus, to a society increasingly obsessed with avoiding emotional risk, sexual passion, despite being secretly envied and longed for by most, is becoming the pariah of emotions.

This is a mistake and renders barren the complex human psyche.

When passion is unbridled, and I believe it should definitely be unbridled if it is to have meaning and portent, it *is* risky and does occasionally mean paying an emotional price. And although such risk appears to be neither valuable nor beneficial in these practical days, all passionate people know instinctively that it is actually both.

So a book such as *Women & Passion*, which explores, explains and ponders the breadth and depth of female passion in all its nuances, contradictions and glory, is a welcome teacher and inspiration in these times. I hope that *Women & Passion* will encourage women to unleash their fettered feelings and discover that without passion in life, there is no life.

—Valerie Gibson, sex and relationship columnist and author, *An Older Woman's Guide to Younger Men*

INTRODUCTION
MY CRISIS OF PASSION

This is a book that arose from my own "crisis of passion," a time in my life when I had lost my centre. I had turned 35, had been married for 10 years, and was working on too many projects for one human being, a hazard of being a writer. My wardrobe consisted of sloppy T-shirts, spandex leggings and baggy sweaters. One day, a handsome younger man made it clear that he was interested in me. I wrestled with whether to stray, and ultimately chose to remain technically faithful. I was feeling fat, old and haggard; he told me I was beautiful, glowing and—a pièce de résistance—"not fat." Within 10 minutes, I was madly in love with someone I didn't know. I lost 10 pounds in 10 days simply because I was too high to eat. I walked around feeling raw and attractive, as though someone had unleashed a beast within me. I bought new clothes; I dyed my hair. I had transformed. People who hadn't seen me for six months didn't recognize me. I wanted to travel, dance and ditch all my projects and responsibilities for fun and adventure. I felt I was ripening. My husband thought I was going through a phase and grunted his disapproval at my behaviour, telling me I wasn't acting my age.

The relationship with the young man deteriorated into one big package of pain: I was the "safe" older woman he felt good about flattering, and felt flattered to have captured; he became the focus of all my passions and desires but remained unavailable. It was a horrible, messy downward spiral that finally ended when I asked myself the right question: How did this situation *become* this situation if I'm so happily married? The answer was simple: I wasn't happy. I had somehow confused "not miserable" with "being happy." But it was too late to go back: the passions had stirred.

The embarrassingly clichéd situation I found myself in made me face deep feelings of longing, unmet desires and emotions I thought I had said goodbye to in my teens and early 20s. "I'm evolved," I told myself. "I can handle these feelings." Some of these feelings were related to facing my age, and all the feelings women go through when they *feel* they are aging and losing their youth, beauty, and ultimately, their sense of power. Some of these feelings had to do with grieving for lost opportunities, or opportunities I only thought were lost. I felt that I was in the midst of being consumed by my own desires.

When I realized I couldn't satisfy my desires within the framework my husband and I had built together, I realized what I had done: I had made the great Economic Trade. I had traded passion for security. I had married a friend and business partner, not a lover. When I was cold and lonely in my early 20s, and a nice warm sweater came along, I grabbed the sweater. Should I have held out for a partner that brought out my passions and desires? The question is moot because at that time I needed that security in order to build my life. Had I not built economic security into my existence then, I may not have had the luxury to question whether I was truly happy. Many of you have done the same thing. It's what a lot of women do. But when the questioning of the status quo starts, passions stir, and the longing begins, some of us need to make changes to satisfy what no longer can be denied.

My crisis of passion was a turning point in my adult life, and it forced me to confront unmet needs. When I gave myself permission to desire more, the messiness of the crisis began to clear, and I was able to see the mistakes as opportunities for growth and opportunities for change. When I realized I'd made the Trade, I knew I had to make the Change. There were great rewards. But there were also great costs.

I began to research other women's choices about passion, and to interview them about the reasons for their choices. The answers took me back to my feminist sociology texts: I began to understand the feminist adage "The personal is political." In other words, through one woman's personal experience with passion is the story of all women's struggles with passion. To illustrate this, I've peppered this book with the experiences lived by women artists, politicians, celebrities and scientists, as well as women I've interviewed (I have given them fictional names).

In this book you'll find collective regrets, mistakes and epiphanies about passion. What, for example, does Eleanor Roosevelt have in common with other women struggling with body image? (Roosevelt, the principal author of the Declaration of Human Rights, actually regretted not being prettier.) What can we learn from the experiences of Ali MacGraw, who gave up a promising career for actor Steve McQueen, an alcoholic, violent and possessive man, only to be left with nothing at the age of 40 but the clothes on her back? How many choices for and against passion can we count within the one life of Elizabeth Taylor, who has said that she "married her affairs"? If you can recognize yourself in the lives of others, you can begin to integrate your own choices about passion and see that you are not alone.

In my own journey I discovered not only that I required passion in my life, but that passion was a requirement for a full life. When I thought more carefully about passion, I recognized that the social history of women had everything to do with women's choices about passion: women trade passion for security, and we do this because of unjust social arrangements that still exist for women. Women are led to believe that there is a payoff for this trade; but many women, like me, discover in their 30s and 40s that the economic rewards of the trade are not worth the emotional flatness they suffer, which often manifests as depression. The consequences of this are put best by Betty Friedan, in the opening paragraph to her 1963 book, *The Feminine Mystique:*

> The problem lay buried, unspoken, for many years in the minds of American women. It was a strange stirring, a sense of dissatisfaction, a yearning that women suffered in the middle of the twentieth century in the United States. Each suburban wife struggled with it alone. As she made the beds, shopped for groceries, matched slipcover material, ate peanut butter sandwiches with her children, chauffeured Cub Scouts and Brownies, lay beside her husband at night—she was afraid to ask even of herself the silent question—'Is this all?' (Friedan:15).

Suppressed passions and desires can also manifest as eating disorders and obsessions: overeating, bingeing and purging are all expressions of suppressed passions, while anorexia nervosa is a disease in which passions are under strict control. Addiction is another way in which suppressed passions are expressed, while other women may wander into abusive relationships because they are attracted to the passion that characterizes such unions. These relationships follow a predictable pattern of the Honeymoon Cycle and Violence Cycle. During the Honeymoon Cycle, the partner is often intensely passionate, romantic and sexually satisfying—particularly when apologizing for a violent episode.

Whether women indulge their passions or suppress them, there are consequences. Our emotions are intricately linked to our conscious choices and unconscious behaviours regarding our passions. This is a book about the passion continuum. If you're looking for the recipe for becoming passionate, you won't find it here; but you might be able to find the ingredients you need to make changes about your passion choices. This book explains what passion is, the ways it manifests, the consequences of suppressing passion and the benefits of consciously harnessing passion for a richer, fuller and more satisfying life. In short, this is a book that will help you understand where your passions lie, and help you decide whether you want to unpack them, unleash them or just let 'em lie there.

THE MEANING OF PASSION

Passion—which we identify with happiness, joy and sexual fulfillment—comes from an ironic root: from the Latin *passio*, which means *suffering*. Gail Sheehy, author of *Passages*, observed that behind every great woman is a little girl who has suffered. How is it that passion arises through suffering? Well, what would you say if I told you that researching passion takes us into the exploration of end-of-life/death-and-dying issues? Those of you who are Christian may recall the phrase "the Passion of Christ"—something I felt compelled to research in light of this topic.

The word "passion" has lost its true meaning for so many of us experiencing a flatness of feeling in our culture. It's been equated with sexual intensity, which may be a feature of passion, but by no means defines it. Without an exploration of end-of-life issues, I could not have understood what I needed to understand to write this book. I wish I could say I willingly explored end-of-life issues, but this is not the case. I was thrown into looking at death quite accidentally.

You see, while working on this book, I was forced to watch my 36-year-old best friend lose a husband of the same age to advanced cancer. Within four months, they went from a normal life to a palliative care unit. I watched my friend hold her husband's hand through breakthrough pain; wipe his forehead of profuse sweating, characteristic of end-stage illness; and simply be with him completely and unconditionally. Actually, she is the only woman in my age group I know who completed her marriage: till death do us part.

My friend was a reserved person, who didn't like to let people in or show emotions; she led a relatively sheltered existence, where her children were safe and no real trauma or suffering had touched her life. Suddenly she was confronted with the essence of life: real feelings, real suffering and raw emotions that could not be covered up anymore. In all the years I had known her, I had never seen her cry. Now she was crying and living on a sort of edge or cliff, waiting for the unknown, and calling on all her inner reserves and strength to get through this experience.

All of the people in this couple's circle were brought to a new rawness, too. We were reminded of the precariousness of life, and how planning for the future cannot replace living in the present. "Feeling your life" is how I would define passion after living through this experience with my friend. And nothing is more passionate, I realized, than dying, or being with someone who is dying.

Living in North America, we rarely talk about death, or see it as inevitable. We're too busy trying to live longer, look younger and research miracle cures for disease. But people die every day. How come we don't know anything about dying until it's happening? The character Morrie in Mitch Albom's *Tuesdays With Morrie* says: "When you know how to die, you know how to live."

FEELING OUR MORTALITY

When we feel our mortality, we "feel our lives." As we age, we become particularly aware of our mortality—especially when someone our own age is dying. But there are other markers of our mortality that may bring us closer to our deaths, and hence, our feelings and our lives. For example, many women "feel" their age on birthdays ending in 5 or 0; or when their youngest child marks an occasion of adulthood, such as graduation, moving out and marriage; or when they watch their parents age, become feeble or disabled; or when they realize that they are not being "seen" as a woman in their aging bodies (not being noticed by men anymore, for example, comes in various experiences for women). One woman who recently turned 60 told me that she began to realize within the last year or so that she could not get service the way she used to. Male servers in restaurants ignored her; male retailers ignored her when she was in a store. She used the term "non-person" to describe how turning 60 made her feel.

When we experience illness or physical vulnerability, our life takes on a new meaning, and we begin to look at it differently. Gail Sheehy refers to this as a the "task of reflection." It is often upon this reflection (Did we live well? Are we happy? Were we good people? Are there things we still want or need to do?) that we become more passionate, but this usually results when we make a conscious shift to another stage of life. At this stage in life, our health, for example, suddenly becomes very important to us; many people become active for the first time, or dramatically change their lifestyle habits—eating well or quitting smoking.

The death of others also affects us differently as we age because it mirrors our progression towards this inevitable event. In fact, Sheehy defines the word "progress" as a series of little victories over little deaths. Writer Virginia Woolf referred to "moments of being" in which we find clarity before returning to the details of everyday life.

Feeling our mortality may sound ominous, but if you didn't know you were going to die one day, you would not find enjoyment in anything you did. There would be no "last piece of cake" sense of time, sense of something being over. There would be no meaningful sex, either, as the sexual experience is a microcosm of the stages of life, ending in what the French call *le petit mort* or "little death"—their term for orgasm. Nor would there be that "last night" on a vacation. Without these small, daily reminders that we will not last forever, our lives would, in fact, be devoid of meaning. At the same time, without endings, there would be no beginnings. There would be nothing new, such as a new food to taste or new places to explore. Without a sense of the new there would be no value in art, or the artist, as it is the uniqueness and newness of an artist's work that we appreciate and place value in. Without feeling our deaths, we cannot feel our lives, you see.

In my own life, I have often been scolded by friends and loved ones for working too much, or too hard. I am told that I am a workaholic, when, in fact, I feel this is an untrue statement. But when I explored the reasons why I produce at the rate I do, I realized it had to do with "feeling" my mortality. Having cancer at an early age—a treatable cancer at the age of 20—impacted my life in ways I hadn't explored until I began working on this book. Because I've been ill, and have faced the prospect of my own death, I have a sense of urgency about my work. If I knew I would live forever, I would not be as concerned with my deadlines or productivity. In this way, I am not unique. Women face their mortality when they make all sorts of decisions that, ostensibly, do not seem to have anything to do with death, such as:

- Sacrificing for their children (this choice is driven by the sense that the children are the future, and that by ensuring children's happiness, life will have meaning and purpose after your death);

- Choosing to go back to school or retrain for a different profession (this choice is driven by a feeling that there are still things to do, or to learn before we die);

- Choosing fertility treatments when conception cannot occur naturally (this choice is driven by an urgency to leave a genetic mark behind);

- Choosing cosmetic surgeries to look younger (this choice is driven by a sense that time is running out on our youth, and we're not ready to age yet);

- Choosing to leave a stagnant relationship or marriage (this choice is driven by the "Is this all" question); or

- Choosing to stay in a less than satisfactory relationship in order to have a child (this choice is also driven by our need to leave a genetic mark on the world).

Why we appreciate beauty

For the most part, beauty does not last, which is why we appreciate it as much as we do. When Diana, former Princess of Wales, was killed in a car crash Labour Day weekend, 1997, the world went into a state of shock. People from all over the world travelled to London to leave flowers or a card or just "be there." News coverage was continuous, and some news stations called upon psychologists and clergy to help explain why there was such a profound sense of loss over her death. I, too, mourned her death and would inexplicably burst into tears each time I heard Elton John's ode to her played on the radio. I was not a Royal Watcher, however, and was at a loss to explain my reaction. When Mother Teresa died a week later, the Western world was not as moved by her death. In fact, there was barely a reaction beyond what was politically correct. Intellectually, we know that Mother Teresa's contributions outweighed Diana's. Yet we did not mourn the loss of Mother Teresa in the same way. Why?

The answer is not complicated: when something beautiful ends, or ends too soon, such as a young, promising life, we profoundly appreciate the meaning of that ending; it is a reminder of our own vulnerability. We are vulnerable to damage; we can die at any time. In Diana's case, we were upset by both a life interrupted and a death that was unnecessary. But for the reckless driving of Diana's vehicle, we reason, she would not have died. Her demise seemed so senseless.

In Elton John's ode Diana was symbolized by a rose, as it has to do with why we appreciate something that has such a short life. Consider the experience of Barbara, when she talks about the death of her 7-year-old son, and the meaning it gave her life:

> When my son died of leukemia, I couldn't tolerate it. I felt as though my life was robbed of meaning and purpose, and I was desperate for a reason for my son's death. *Why did he have to die?* I went to see my priest, hoping for some answers, and he told me something that has since allowed me to carry on. He told me that we must always appreciate something beautiful in this world because we cannot know how long it will be with us. He compared my son to a beautiful flower that graced the earth for a short time. The lesson of my son's death for me, he said, was to especially appreciate the gift of life, and what I perceive, sense and feel on the physical world while I am still alive. He told me that just because my son's time on this earth was shorter than mine doesn't mean his life was not meaningful. The length of a life is not important; it is the essence of the life that is.

When something beautiful ends too soon, we experience this as tragedy. But it is through tragedy that we find meaning. This is often a universal experience when we live through the death of a child:

> One of the early lessons of Michael's dying had to do with the nature of tragedy. At first glance, his dying appeared to be a horrible tragedy: a little boy with no childhood or future was suffering and dying from something totally beyond anyone's control. But his own and his family's suffer-

ing shrank compared with the joy and growth he engendered. While Michael's illness and dying were tragic, they were not *only* tragic. What we experienced was far greater and far richer than sorrow alone...

While the electrical storms in Michael's brain grew worse, the love around him grew stronger. People who had known him through the Medicaid office or his preschool formed a constant stream of visitors. Virtual strangers to [Michael's father] would drop by the house, introducing themselves and their connection to Michael, and ask if they could sit with him for a few hours. As I witnessed this parade of pilgrims, I marveled at how Michael's dying belied medical wisdom. His chart and medical history—the description of a boy with a hopeless illness whose life was a litany of misery and debilitation—looked like only tragedy. Yet when I removed the medical filters from my eyes, I was struck by how powerfully his life was affecting his family and friends and by the loving relationships he inspired. (Byock, *Dying Well*: 175, 186)

Our appreciation of beauty explains a myriad of activities, such as birdwatching, taking nature walks, enjoying thunderstorms and wanting "rooms with a view." For women, the appreciation of beauty frequently leads to devastating consequences. When it is the beautiful, youthful woman who is appreciated and valued in our society, a woman not considered beautiful or a woman who is losing her beauty to aging, is devalued. Often, this leads women into destructive or self-sacrificing behaviours in the name of "beauty preservation."

Dieting, for example, is a complex behaviour that gets tangled up with beauty preservation, as well as denial of pleasure, both related to feeling our mortality. Delicious food would not be as pleasurable to us if we were immortal; at the same time, if food was not pleasurable, or meaningful, then denying ourselves food would have no meaning, either. Food refusal, in essence, is an act of food *appreciation*.

THE MEANING OF LIFE

The meaning of life is the meaning of death. Without death, there would be no meaning to our lives; but without a meaningful life, our deaths would have no meaning, either. It's a Catch 22. Thus, passion is the act of feeling our lives by appreciating our future, and eventual, death.

To understand meaningfulness in life and death, it's useful to compare the experiences of two deaths. First, consider the death of Martha's great-aunt Nora:

Nora was a pretty miserable woman, and miserable to be around. She was cheap, if not miserly, with her great wealth (which, rumour has it, she and her late husband acquired by cheating her own brother in business); she had no children (she had adopted two children who were Holocaust survivors in the late 1940s but "gave them back" because they were too much trouble). She also had no great affection for extended-family members, and hence, no extended-family members had great affection for her. She had no real friends; they were merely window-dressing plastic relationships from her bridge groups or golf resorts. In essence, she contributed nothing to anyone's life—including a mere compliment. She had problems with everyone; this one was too X; that one was too Y.

I had the unfortunate position of being one of her only blood relatives in town, and felt obliged to care for her in her dying days, along with another great-niece, who was caught in a similar position. When Nora died, there were less than 10 people at her funeral; one of them was Nora's 90-year-old sister, who hadn't spoken to her since the 1930s (they had had a falling-out). In the Jewish tradition, you need eight men to be pallbearers. There were not enough pallbearers, and the funeral home had to provide "fillers." The scene was so pathetic, we all burst into tears.

The eulogy was worse. In her 87 years on this earth, all that could be said, in truth, is that she was a good golfer. She is not missed by anyone. And even through her will, she managed to bitterly divide family members by leaving money to some nieces and nephews and excluding others. (In one case, she left six figures to a wealthy niece and nothing to the poor one; in another case, she left seven figures to a fluff charity, but nothing to another impoverished niece with a little boy, who had been good to Nora.) Nora was in death what she was in life: mean and nasty.

Compare the above to Ira Byock's description of his dying father, in *Dying Well:*

There was little for us to do, and none of us wanted to leave his side. This time felt sacred, but not in the way that scripture, liturgy, or chants are sacred. There was a luminous— or numinous—quality to the moment. A great man was passing. So much was being lost, but oh, what a treasure he was. What a privilege to have known him, to have loved and been loved by him and to have been raised by him.

As we sat around his bed and sipped coffee through the long hours of that last night, Mom and I told old Byock family stories... Sleeplessness had left us emotionally defenseless, and our shared sadness contributed to a bleary camaraderie. We cried in sadness but also in joy...

I had grown accustomed to seeing death through medical eyes; my father's cancer forced me to experience terminal illness from the vantage point of a patient's family. Furthermore, through my father's eyes, I glimpsed dying from the point of view of a person living in the shadow of death. Dad's dying was certainly not the happiest time in our family's life, but as a family we had never been more open, or more openly loving. His illness allowed us, I could say forced us, to talk about the things that mattered: family, our relationships with one another, our shared past, and the unknown future. We reminisced about good times and bad, we cried, and we laughed. We apologized for a host of transgressions, and we granted, and were granted, forgiveness. Through Dad's illness and in his dying, we all grew individually and together. (Byock: 23–26)

In *Dying Well*, Byock talks about what a revelation it was to him that good deaths existed outside the romantic realms of poetry, fiction or religious literature. Every so often, he says, a family would come to see him after a patient died and describe their loved one's passing as extraordinary. Through our deaths, we can also transform our lives, as Byock describes through one dying patient's experience:

> By finally allowing himself to be immersed in sadness, he moved through his suffering, emerging beyond it into the arms of his family. In so doing he achieved a paradoxical wellness in his dying. In the end, his suffering became a catalyst for dying well... All his life, anger had been his reaction to disappointment and frustration; this emotion was familiar territory to him. He had no training in sadness, no experience with it. Sadness was an absolute unknown and thus terrifying. When he was forced to confront his sadness, he finally took that first step off the diving board and realized, as frightening as it was, that he could enter the darkness and survive. Once he was able to cry and to acknowledge the depth of his own sadness, it lost its power. He was changed by the experience, but somehow more whole. (Byock: 82–84)

THE PASSION OF CHRIST

When I observed the passion of death through my friend's dying husband's experience, I realized something about the

Passion of Christ. Since I am not a Christian, thinking about Jesus Christ was not something I did on a regular basis. But I imagined him on the cross. He was naked. He was in pain. He was being watched by others, and feeling humiliation and loss of dignity. This understanding was validated for me by a priest and palliative care specialist. It is the vulnerability and rawness of Christ's experience on the cross that we now see in palliative care units every day.

The traditional interpretation of the Passion of Christ is one of hope. It is more typically an Easter story: because Easter celebrates Christ's resurrection, through his suffering comes meaning, growth or redemption. This "hope through suffering" concept is pretty ancient across all religions, but in this case it was developed in response to the problem of suffering from a Christian perspective—How are Christians to respond to the threat of their own personal suffering and death? The story of Christ's transcendence of real human suffering is perhaps the most fundamental and important aspect of the Christian faith. In the Christian faith, the icon of Christ on the cross is a reminder of what it means to be human—to suffer and struggle.

It can be argued that by "feeling" his life, Christ transcended it. Morrie, in Mitch Albom's *Tuesdays With Morrie*, says much the same thing in his "when you know how to die, you know how to live" statement. Christians are taught, therefore, to be "compassionate"—to co-suffer (with Christ, for example)—and they, too will transcend, or grow. Compassion is considered an important aspect of Christianity because when we become more sensitive to the suffering of others, we value our own human experiences all the more.

Women, passion
and the Passion of Christ

If redemption is the hopeful part of the story of Christ, women tend to identify with the darker side: the crucified Christ, or the suffering Christ. What does the Passion of Christ have to do with women and passion? Are women, on some level, doing a Passion Play of the crucifixion? The experience of being female mirrors the experience of crucifixion:

- *Vulnerability.* Since women are objects of beauty in our culture, their appearance and body image is vulnerable to onlookers, and can be attacked. We feel looked at and naked when we are in public. We feel ridiculed when we are not meeting the beauty standard.

- *Bleeding or "open wounds."* When we menstruate, we are bleeding. In many cultures, women experience genital mutilation, and are left "bleeding and raw" for a lifetime. Women may also self-mutilate, by cutting themselves, piercing themselves. Childbirth and menopause—our life-changing experiences—are also public and "bloody" events.

- *Betrayal.* In many of our social experiences, we feel betrayed by unjust social arrangements that exist for women in our culture. We can be abused sexually or have violent acts perpetrated upon us because we are weaker and more vulnerable. When we love, we can experience betrayal through unfaithful partners, which in today's culture can lead to our deaths through sexually transmitted diseases such as HIV/AIDS.

- *Martyrdom.* Women typically sacrifice their own needs for someone else's, such as their child's or partner's. And women's moral decisions are more likely to be based on who will be affected by the decision rather than on their own needs. For example, studies show that regardless of how strongly opposed to, or in favour of, abortion a woman is, she bases the decision on how it will affect the relationships around her, rather than on herself. How will her husband, or existing children, feel about a new baby? If the new baby will threaten those relationships, even a woman morally opposed to abortion may decide to terminate. On the other hand, if she does not want another baby, a woman may keep it rather than upset the relationships around her. In other words, who her choice will affect is the deciding factor in making the choice.

WOMEN AND SUFFERING

First of all, we suffer because we are aware. The more awareness we have about our lives, the more we suffer. All human beings suffer; it is part of what it means to be human and to grow. But there are different kinds of suffering human beings endure, and more specifically, different kinds of suffering women endure that may not lead to growth but to a diminished quality of life. Physical pain, for example, can trigger suffering that doesn't necessarily lead to emotional growth.

Every month, millions of women on this planet endure menstrual pain; millions of women are beaten by spouses, boyfriends, parents; millions of women are sexually abused or subjected to painful rituals such as female genital mutilation that cause them lifelong physical pain and suffering. Emotional trauma linked to the physical pain can be seen as an extension of the physical event. The memory of sexual abuse is a reliving of real, physical pain, for example, as well as emotional pain from the experience. But not all suffering from physical pain leads to sadness: childbirth is painful, yet joyful for many women. The pain and suffering are there, but the memories often fade as the joyousness of the birth transcends it.

Then there is the suffering we endure in the absence of any physical pain, as in experiencing the death of a loved one, or empathizing with a loved one who is ill. A mother watching her child suffer, for example, is not in any physical pain, but still suffers.

Suffering can develop when we realize our lives or situations are not improving, or when they are declining. Stagnating, or being in a rut, or finding your life is getting worse rather than better, are conditions that lead to suffering. Once our basic needs (safety, food, shelter, love) are looked after, we are driven toward self-actualization. When our life circumstances stymie self-actualization or spiritual growth, we suffer. The longing for material possessions, money or an intimate relationship is often just an expression of longing for self-realization. Later in life many of us also begin to question our attachments to material possessions and power, and as we get older, begin to see the difference between real needs (love, friendship, respect) and artificial needs (money, power, prestige).

For those of us who like the status quo and our quality of life, suffering can develop when a life event of some kind threatens our status quo, our identity or selfhood, or our quality of life. The threat can come from an infinite variety of sources, of course, ranging from physical illness to financial hardship.

Can suffering be good for you?

Ira Byock observes: Clinicians who are adept at working with dying persons know from experience that, in the midst of profound suffering, not only comfort, but also triumph and exhilaration, are possible. The separation between suffering and the sense of growth and transformation is but a membrane (Byock: 246).

Indeed, suffering can have a positive outcome. In other words, no pain, no gain! When you're in a rut, or feel trapped by life's circumstances, the suffering you feel can be your mind's and body's way of saying: "Wake up and change!" In this case, the only way to stop the suffering is to change the conditions of your life (as in leaving a stagnant marriage) or at least change the way you view the conditions of your life (as in "My infertility isn't a curse after all—it's actually allowed me to go back to school and change professions). In other words, if you can't change your life, you can still change your perspective on it, which can be a huge life-changing event, even though the conditions of your life remain the same.

When it is your body that is triggering your suffering, the process of disease and illness frequently leads to a new and evolved perspective on life. On an emotional level, growth has been compared to peeling an onion: the more you peel, the more you cry. Confronting fears, falling in love, falling out of love, examining painful memories—are all experiences that trigger emotional growth and maturity.

Suffering that doesn't lead to personal growth, or illumination (which often occurs in the face of mortality, aging, terminal illness) is probably a good definition of hell. Why suffer unless something better will result from it? Indeed, suffering may not yield immediate tangible results. An interesting concept is one which Talmudic scholars call the "hiding face of God"—a popular argument used by many religious scholars to deal with the problem of evil. (If a good, kind God exists, why is there so much evil in the world?) The argument goes something like this: since the lifespan of one human being is so short, compared to the lifespan of the human race (or God), it's not always possible to understand why God "hides its face" when individual humans appear to be suffering needlessly; there may be a good reason for our suffering, but we won't live long enough to understand the outcome. For example, a mouse used in cancer research would be suffering without the knowledge that its suffering is contributing to a cancer cure, which, in fact, will prevent the suffering of millions of people in the future.

Many women appear to suffer for no good reason. But if you are aware that you are suffering, you are living, in fact, a passionate existence. If you can learn something new, feel something new or change direction as a result of your suffering, you're growing, and this is an indication that you are alive, and part of the human race; it means you are feeling your life—something that passionate people do.

Disconnection, women and suffering

The large body of work that looks at causes of sadness and depression in women shows us that women suffer most when they are feeling out of connection with the world around them. Women in healthy relationships gain strength and meaning from their connections. Connectedness brings women increased zest, well-being and motivation; connection allows them to act positively within their relationships; it brings them increased self-knowledge and awareness of "the other" (family, friends and colleagues); connection brings them increased self-worth, as well as a desire to make more connections. As one article on women and connection states: "Being in connection means to be emotionally accessible. And this means to be vulnerable."

Betty shares an eerie yet common tale of a woman in disconnection whose experience shows us what we can attract when we are desperate for connection:

> My marriage was secure, but I was feeling really out of touch with my husband. I guess I was looking for something outside my marriage to fill me up. I started to volunteer at a local food bank, which gave me a sense of belonging. But because I guess I was so desperate to connect, my judgment about people was impaired. I met "Deborah" at the food bank. Deborah appeared to be suffering from a breakup of a relationship, and was sharing her life details with me. It seemed as though we shared similar pain, and were eager to bond. Soon we were like "sisters" sharing our lives,

emotions, and in my case, some compromising information about people I loved and cared about, including a man I was longing to have an affair with—the husband, in fact, of another food bank volunteer (they were volunteering as a husband-and-wife team).

The more unhappy I became in my husband's company, and the more unlikely it seemed that I could capture the affections of the man I "really" wanted, the more I yearned to talk to Deborah, and share or escape. Deborah told me she was good friends with the man I wanted, and told me that the feelings were mutual; he, too, wanted an affair apparently. Deborah appeared to be rather unbalanced in her own emotions, but I didn't care how unbalanced she seemed as long as I felt heard.

Then, the most unimaginable event occurred: Deborah, as it turned out, was, in fact, not at all the caring individual she appeared to be. She was, all the while, fabricating stories about me to others—including the man I wanted. For example, she was telling people that I was an hysteric who was threatening her; she distorted facts to other volunteers based on very private information I had disclosed, and then stole my credit card and incurred debt.

It took me months of standing tall through the rumour mill before it became evident to all who knew Deborah that she was a pathological liar. Other volunteers in the organization were equally harmed by her. But by the time the truth came out, it was too late.

I blamed myself for the episode, and couldn't bear that I was so disconnected from intimacy with my husband that I would "sell my soul" for the feeling of being connected to *someone,* and the thrill of being privy to what turned out to be completely false information. My husband found out about "the creature"—what I call Deborah. And he actually accused me of risking his life and safety because I couldn't resist "gossiping like a 17-year old." He feared that if I reported the credit card theft, Deborah might stalk us (she had a criminal record of this, actually), or even accuse him of rape. The experience left me frightened of connecting with new people because I felt I couldn't trust my instincts.

Betty's story is not unlike what Monica Lewinsky attracted into her life via Linda Tripp, when she, too, was in obvious disconnection with the world around her. I'm sure Monica disclosed what she did to Linda because she needed to feel some validation, but her emotional openness left her open to attack. I noted with interest that female public sympathy lay with Monica, which has enabled her to pick up the pieces of her life. We sympathize with Monica because we have all been "tripped up" by Lindas in our lives. But when women are yearning for connection with a man, they can attract similar male betrayals, as Carolyn reveals:

I had just left a nine-year relationship and was wide open emotionally. I needed to get some pictures of myself done for a corporate brochure and a co-worker suggested a photographer who apparently did very nice work. When I

went to look at the photographer's book, I immediately felt
a connection with him. We talked about all kinds of things
within the first 30 minutes of meeting. I was excited that
maybe I had found a male friend again—something I hadn't
had in a long time. At first, everything seemed like a normal
friendship. The photographer called me frequently, and I
took his initiation of a friendship as an invitation to disclose.
I was feeling open and easy about disclosing my feelings,
experiences and all the messy parts of my life in a
completely unguarded fashion. I was also feeling very
"messy," which made my disclosures all the more compromising; I thought he was disclosing in a similar fashion to
me. But one day, out of the blue, he abruptly ended a phone
call by cutting me off and telling me I was "boring" him,
and that he would not be calling me again. His behaviour
was so bizarre, I thought he was kidding. He then used
details from my disclosures to attack me as a way to prove
that I was substandard friendship material. Stunned and
hurt, I was speechless. "Well, Carolyn," he said, "we just
don't have anything left to talk about." It felt as though I had
been raped and invaded—what on earth had I allowed into
my soul? To open up and then be dismissed—just like that.
I remember feeling like I had been punched in the stomach.
There was a misogynistic, violent edge to it all.

A few days later, he called back and apologized, admitting
that he had a problem with connection with women, and
that this was his pathetic pattern: he would cut off the relationship when his passions were stirred by a woman, even
though he longed to connect to her. He was eager to try

again and forge ahead, but the same pattern kept repeating until I realized I had let a very dangerous and destructive force into my life. The experience left me jaded and disappointed in myself for letting him in.

A lot of our suffering comes from our yearning for connection. Vulnerability can, of course, lead us to be taken advantage of. Most women have a few bitter experiences of their vulnerability and openness when they've allowed less than savoury characters into their lives. A lot of us may stray into relationships with men who take terrible advantage of our feelings and openness. The problem with vulnerability is that it cannot be halfway. Thus, when women open up to someone, and truly connect, they risk being vulnerable, and they risk suffering as a result, when that connection is not authentic, or when it is not respected.

Women may also self-sabotage their connections when they fear they are feeling too much, and are not sure their feelings will be reciprocated, respected or returned. There is simply no way around this risk. This is why women learn to shut down; this is when passion becomes repressed. In my own painful lessons with connection and disconnection, I learned to embrace my vulnerability and openness, for without risking connection, I cannot connect at all. My vulnerability is my strength; it is also my greatest weakness. But when I am vulnerable, I feel.

In this chapter, we essentially learned the answer to the age-old question what is the meaning of life by exploring

*the meaning of passion. As you can see, however, passion
can be painful, which causes us to shut down or repress it.*

*The next chapter looks at an underreported phenomenon
many women experience at a certain time in their lives,
which I call the "ripening." This is a combination of physical and emotional signs that can trigger the bubbling
forth of repressed passions. Many of you may recognize
yourselves in the next chapter, which can hopefully vali-
date what many women feel as a troubling yet potentially
exciting time in their lives.*

2

RIPENING
WHEN PASSIONS STIR

The term "ripening" is one I have coined to describe what happens when there is a passionate awakening or stirring in the bodies and souls of women as they pass their thirtieth birthdays. For some women, these stirrings start to bubble as early as age 30. In my case, I was 34 when I felt the first stirrings, only to be shocked by an explosion of uncontrollable passions that coincided with my thirty-fifth birthday. Many women feel these stirrings a little later, around 38 or 39, or in their 40s. Sexual researchers refer to women "peaking" in their 30s and 40s.

What I'm describing is more than sexual peaking. What I call ripening is coupled with intensely feeling one's mortality. I recall telling people at the time that I felt like "a ripe, luscious piece of fruit that needed to be picked *now*—not tomorrow or the next day but *now!*" (In the June 2000 issue of *More*, actress Sela Ward, 43, describes herself as feeling like "a juicy piece of fruit.") Ripening, of course, also implies that there is a rot that follows. Ripening implies an aging to perfection that needs to be tasted immediately. There is an urgency to the urges. During my ripening, I could actually feel my skin peeling and renewing itself; feel my breasts becoming rounder; feel my body effortlessly becoming thinner yet more shapely. On one occasion, after I made love with my partner, we kept feeling my skin because it felt smoother and silkier than it did an hour prior to lovemaking. Was it the sweat? The heat? What was going on?

Everywhere I went, I could feel men staring, and I was profoundly aware of their scents. I kept asking my girlfriends, "Are you smelling men more than usual?" I expected to be laughed at, but strangely enough, the response was usually: "You, too? I thought it was just me!" Many of my friends were also experiencing powerful urges to have another baby, which was met with protest from their partners. In my case, whenever I encountered men—on street corners, elevators, conferences, stores—and particularly, Fedex delivery men—I was keenly aware of each unique scent; their colognes would be mixed with their body odours, creating an almost intoxicating aroma. The scent would start my flow. Not menstrual flow, but literally a flow of sexual juices—the most accurate term, really. (My lover called me his river.) At night, heat would travel through my torso, and my lover would actually display shock at the amount of heat coming off my body. In Ayervedic medicine, this is known as the kundilini, or sexual energy that is unleashed.

Writing about my ripening now, it sounds erotic and exciting. But going through the first stages of the experience, without information or knowledge about what was going on, was terrifying. I actually thought I was losing my mind. And my behaviour was wildly erratic, which did not help as my marriage was breaking up. For example, in January, my husband and I had decided that we would separate in a calm manner. We would simply sell the house in the spring, and live as roommates until it was sold. Life would have been a lot less complicated for me had I simply followed that plan. Instead, when I met a man in March, on a Monday, before the house was put up for sale, it seemed like a perfectly good idea to flee my house and move in with him by Wednesday. (I moved out three months later.) I had found my "passion playmate." He was game for anything and so was I. We exhausted each other within a couple of weeks. I never knew my body was capable of such manoeuvres, pleasures, secretions and convulsions. The fact that all this was happening beyond my thirty-fifth birthday was shocking to me; I felt my best, my youngest in years. And it showed.

My sister was concerned about the demise of my personal life. I told her: "All I know is that when I have 21 orgasms in one night, I don't *care* what a mess my life is in." My sister was quiet. I thought she was going to lecture me about getting counselling.

"You had 21 orgasms in one night... *21?*"

"Wait a minute... maybe it was 23... I lost count."

"And you're still *alive?*"

Thankfully, older friends verified that I was not going crazy. One of my friends in her late 40s said: "Yep, that thirty-fifth birthday is a bitch, huh?" My mother (who was divorced by that age, too) said she'd felt similar stirrings, and assured me that I was "normal," but declined to give me details about her own experiences. My ripening was validated; I was not alone. Off I went to research the phenomenon, which not only inspired this chapter, but my exploration into the subject of passion.

THE PHENOMENON OF RIPENING

As a medical health journalist, who has written about the biological stirrings of women in each reproductive stage and age, I found myself having to put on my sociologist hat to understand what was going on in my own ripening. And through interviews with other women, I discovered something that is so universal, yet so underreported, it begs exploration, dialogue and debate. First, ripening is as much a phenomenon as it is a process. Ripening is much more than simply a sexual peak; it is an awakening of the senses, which comprises our sexuality. Ripening also coincides with a social ripening, a time when women are just beginning to feel secure in their careers, or financially stable. Thus, there are physical and emotional components to the process.

The signs

In the same way that menopause manifests over a period of several years, so does ripening. The signs of ripening include:

- A growing restlessness with the status quo (could be career or marriage). This could manifest as feelings of sadness, depression or avoidance behaviour (oversocializing to avoid going home; drinking.) Many women may psychologically divorce their spouses.

- A resurgence of sexuality, sexual potency or prowess. This is different than puberty; this "resurrection" is accompanied by powerful feelings of desire not just for sex but for intimacy and romance. It can manifest as infatuations or relationships with (other) men or women; flirtatious behaviour; affairs or affair-seeking behaviour; and courting excitement—in all its forms (desire to travel, dance, enjoy, spend money). Sexual enjoyment also increases at this time: more profound orgasms, multiple orgasms, excessive vaginal lubrication. (A time when many women purchase vibrators!)

- A powerful feeling of wanting to reproduce. For women with children, this could manifest as wanting to have another child; for women without children, the desire to mate with someone (almost anyone will do!) may be overwhelming; the desire to have a child through self-insemination may also be present if there is no partner.

- A feeling of being more attractive (generally, the feeling is that you're the most attractive you've ever been). This can manifest in sometimes dramatic changes in appearance: weight loss; cosmetic changes (new hairstyle, etc.); wardrobe changes (choosing more body-hugging clothes over baggy, body-hiding clothing); and actually looking radiant—"glowing," "sexy "or "beaming" (as many women in ripening often hear).

- A more profound sense of mortality. This manifests as feeling self-conscious about age; feeling your youth and vitality is about to slip away but hasn't yet; feeling you have a "limited time offer" to really enjoy life!

Ripening coincides with several sociological ripenings too. It is during their 30s and 40s that many women experience:

- Career peaks and perks;

- Upgrading of their education and skills;

- Sufficient sexual experience to feel comfortable in their skin;

- Completing their families (not having any more children);

- Having money (often after many years of struggle); and

- Enjoying independence.

Gail Sheehy refers to second adolescence that women can enjoy in their 30s and 40s. One woman told me that after her divorce, she felt like a "teenager—only this time with money." Sheehy shares a quote from a woman who commented on this:

> Adolescence is so much more fun the second time around. I feel much younger than I did when I was twenty-two and married... .Until I was divorced from my second husband, I could *never imagine* living the rest of my life alone. My mother brought me up that you are defined by being married. I find, on the contrary, I *relish* being single. When both my children were launched at the same time as my second separation, it felt like a huge *liberation*. (Sheehy, *New Passages*: 132)

Ripening manifests with what I call the "stirrings." In my case, my stirring occurred around age 34; many women feel these stirrings a little later, around 38 or 39 or in their 40s. A lot of men in their 20s will deliberately seek out 30-something and 40-something women as sexual partners. It's sort of a best-kept secret that these women make the best partners. It's important to note that my stirrings were very much hetero-sexual, but many women experience ripening as an awakening of their lesbian desires, too, as Denise did:

> I was 37, and living within a traditional marriage. I had entered a midwifery program, and befriended a lesbian colleague, who suddenly kissed me one night when we were out talking. The colleague was frank about her attraction to me; I was somewhat ambivalent, but not entirely turned off. The kiss with another woman aroused deep feelings of passion within me. The kiss was sensual and I would find myself masturbating to its memory. I began to notice other women, and found myself lubricated at the thought of being with other women. I started to explore sex with my lesbian colleague. At first I thought it was just a phase, but the relationship exposed another side of my sexuality. I was able to be myself sexually in the lesbian relationship, something I felt I could not be in my heterosexual relationship with my husband. I eventually moved in with my colleague/lover, but after a few years, began seeing men again. I truly believe all women have lesbian desires that, given the right circumstances, could be awakened.

Studies, in fact, show that there is far more fluidity in female sexuality, but that cultural barriers and stigmatization around lesbianism or bisexuality prevent them from exploring their sexuality with other women. Many scholars in the area of female sexuality and gender maintain that all women have the potential to be lesbian or bisexual, meaning that heterosexuality is only one expression of female sexuality.

My research has shown that some women ripen as late as their 50s and 60s, and it usually coincides, again, with sociological or financial ripenings, as in Linda's case:

> I was 66 when my husband died from complications of Alzheimer's disease. Prior to his Alzheimer's diagnosis, I lived in a very restricted marriage, where he was boss and I felt compelled to obey his every order. Our sex life was unsatisfying, too; I had never had an orgasm in all the years we were married, but in those days it wasn't considered important. After he was diagnosed, my caregiver role consumed all of my time and energy and lasted roughly 10 years.

> When he finally died, I felt sheer freedom. I can't begin to describe how good I felt. The house was paid for long ago, and I did what I wanted, when I wanted. I started to develop interests in everything: trying new restaurants, travelling and taking Tai Chi—something I had always wanted to do. I made friends with a younger woman in my Tai Chi class, and together we went shopping for new clothes. I looked years younger in my new wardrobe, and friends kept telling me I was "glowing." My circle of friends became much

younger, and I experienced an age reversal of sorts. Although I did not begin dating, it was my interest in life and people that peaked. I felt powerful, and sensual, but my upbringing made it difficult for me to let go sexually. (Secretly, I would fantasize about this, though.)

Sometimes the triggers of a ripening are subtle, as Kim tells us:

I was 59 and bitterly dreading my sixtieth birthday. I had not been with a man in over 15 years. One day, a young man on the subway smiled at me in a way that made me feel feminine again. Then I became overwhelmed with wanting to be sexual again. I guess that smile sort of perked me up. I started to care about my appearance, which I hadn't done in years. I got a new haircut, and low-lighted my gray hair. Although I never saw that man again, I kept thinking about him, and wondering if I was normal for actually being attracted to a man young enough to be my son.

Jeanne Beker, host of *FashionTelevision*, and author of the semi-autobiographical *Unbottled*, comments on her own ripening, which she feels is more intense now at 48 (and she felt ripe 10 years ago, too!) than it was even two years ago, when she was married. She says:

I look at all my friends in their 40s and realize there's nothing more attractive than a woman who knows herself—who is interesting and interested in life. And as I age, I just get more interested in life. Everything heightens as we age— sex, a good meal... everything. For our mothers, re-singled lives were miserable, but it's not the same for our generation of re-singled women. One of the most beautiful women (and believe me—I've interviewed them all)—and I mean heads and shoulders above the supermodels—is Ali MacGraw, who is 62. She is still ripening, and I was blown away by her inner beauty and calm, which comes with age and experience. (And you know she's also been doing yoga for a hundred million years!)

Valerie Gibson, 60, who is a sex and relationship columnist for the *Toronto Sun*, and author of *The Older Woman's Guide To Younger Men* told me in an interview: "Young men are a sort of portal through which the older woman can experience something she otherwise wouldn't. You know you won't have it for the rest of your life, but while it's there you can look in and go 'whoo-hoo.'" In her book she writes:

An Older Woman knows sex is exciting, good exercise, releases tension, keeps you fit, keeps you young and feels good. Combine this with a Young Man's enthusiasm, energy, passion and constant readiness, not to mention hard stomach, firm thighs, smooth young skin, and the fact that he always looks good in the morning, no matter what, and you have the Older Woman's ultimate sexual dream. (Gibson: 64, 65)

One of the most interesting ripenings can be seen in the life of Princess Margaret, sister to Queen Elizabeth. Princess Margaret was known for her beauty and her raciness, which gave her the nickname "the rebel princess"—long before Diana and Fergie came along. In the 1970s, when she was 43, Princess Margaret began an almost 10-year relationship with a 25-year-old man she met at a party. When she met him, she had put on weight from a bad marriage to a philandering husband, as well as from her heavy drinking. Within a couple of weeks of meeting her young man, she had slimmed down and was looking absolutely stunning.

Baby fever

The strong desire to reproduce may also be considered a ripening period for many women. They feel ripe for conception, and it is a feeling so powerful it cannot be denied, as Gina shares:

> I am the mother of two, and had reached a stage where I finally had some time to myself. Both my children, at the time 6 and 7, were in school. But each time I saw a baby, I felt these terrible pangs of sadness, and would start to cry. I kept approaching young mothers I saw in public and ask if I could hold their babies. At night I would feel heat in my lower pelvis area, and I would try to initiate sex with my husband, who would usually tell me he was too tired. One night, I forced myself on him, in a very unusual move for me, and demanded that he get me pregnant. But he refused

me, and told me he did not want more children. This issue—
what I call my "baby fever"—came between us, and eventually, we separated.

Sometimes the feeling to reproduce becomes a dangerous,
negative obsession:

> I didn't marry until 40. At 41 I got pregnant naturally, and
> fell madly in love with motherhood. I revelled in the feelings
> that welled up within me when my baby breast-fed. When
> my son turned 2, I wanted another baby. I just "wanted
> more." I couldn't get pregnant, and entered a fertility treat-
> ment program. After three trials of IVF [in vitro fertilization],
> my husband and I had agreed to stop. But I wouldn't. I kept
> signing up for more invasive therapies, and I became
> involved with the infertility community, which my husband
> called "the cult." I just got swept up in the whole infertility
> movement, and actually became a spokeswoman locally for
> the plight of those suffering from secondary infertility.
>
> A lot of women were in the same boat. When people told
> me that I should thank my lucky stars for my one, beautiful
> little boy, it enraged me... I wasn't *finished* with my family,
> and it was incomplete to me. But the irony is that I guess I
> neglected my little boy for my infertility work, which
> angered my husband.
>
> I guess I see secondary infertility as a disease, and believe
> it should be respected as a disease. My husband wouldn't

see things this way, and eventually he left. After a lot of soul-searching I went to China and I guess "bought" a child. Still, I can't help feeling that my body failed me.

The longing for (more) children stems from what Gail Sheehy believes is the most radical voluntary alteration of the life cycle. Until very recently, our species has followed the basic instinct to breed as soon as possible. But contemporary women are forced to delay childbirth for economic as well as cultural reasons. At one time, women could choose between having a career or having a baby. The choice for most women today is whether they will have a baby *and* work, or not have a baby *and* work. How did this happen?

The declining rate of teenage marriage in North America since the 1960s is directly related to the availability of more educational opportunities and career choices for women, as well as a general acceptance of common-law living versus marriage. A decline in blue-collar jobs has led to poor job prospects for young adults without higher education, meaning that more women have had no choice but to enter the blue- or pink-collar workforce.

Younger women are also competing for jobs with older, divorced women, who must work in order to make ends meet. Moreover, the high cost of living has made it virtually impossible for most young adults to afford a family until they're in their mid to late 20s. Therefore, while marriage or family plans are often delayed, intercourse is not. The prospect of "waiting until marriage" becomes more and more unrealistic as marriage seems unaffordable until relatively late in life, or even unlikely to teens growing up in dysfunctional or broken homes. In other words, few women have the luxury to choose between staying home or working. As attitudes about sexuality and women's roles in society have shifted over the last 40 years, marriage rates have declined while sexual activity has increased. So that means fewer couples are willing to commit themselves to a life partner earlier in life, which makes it more difficult for women in their 20s and 30s to find suitable life partners, and results in a further delay in child-bearing; and more casual, unprotected sexual encounters earlier in life have led to an explosion in sexually transmitted diseases (STDs), which can damage reproductive organs (particularly in women), causing infertility in the 30s and 40s.

Reproductive technology also creates the illusion that there is more time for women to have children. Sheehy relates the following story:

> The attractive 48-year-old woman perched on the examining table when the big-city doctor walks in is all blushes and titters. "I know it's absolutely silly, and you're going to yell at me, but I have a fabulous new beau, and we've chosen not to use contraception," she says, looking up coyly at her doctor as she wags a tasseled cowboy boot. "We're just going to ride out the consequences."
>
> "That's one way of dealing with passion," the doctor quips, "as long as you're reasonably comfortable that you're not going to get some dreadful disease."
>
> "Yes, but now my period is late," the woman announces with a maiden's blush.

"Well, you're forty-eight; it's not uncommon, says the doctor.

"I want a test for pregnancy," the woman insists.

"I would always recommend that, but it's far more likely that you're just beginning a more serious manifestation of your perimenopause," the doctor responds matter-of-factly. "It's extremely unlikely that you're going to have a spontaneous pregnancy during this part of your life."

The woman will not be dissuaded by facts; she wants too badly to believe. "But I have a friend who's attempting to conceive with in vitro fertilization," she says defensively, "and she's forty-seven."

The doctor, muting her disbelief, asks the patient, "Is your friend using her own eggs?" The woman seems surprised by the question. "Of course"—as if one should expect a woman in her late forties to have great success in producing. (Sheehy, *New Passages*: 98)

The strong desire for a baby is an expression of the ripening process: the womb is ready *now*. The baby must be conceived *now!* But when there is no father for the baby, or circumstances are not in favour of conception, many women feel tremendous loss, and grieve the loss of a baby and the motherhood fairy tale. For many women, their fertility crisis, which is really a crisis of passion, is the first time they have lost control over their reproductive lives.

The passions that are ignited through "fertility interruptus" can be met with a debilitating life crisis for women, who feel like failures. And again, it is feeling our mortality that is expressed through grieving that occurs with infertility. The drive to reproduce is within all species, and when we age, and have not done so, many women feel incomplete. Childbirth, according to many women, is the most passionate of experiences. What some women don't realize is that after having a baby you still have to raise it. Consider Emma's experience:

> I was in transition in my life, and had just turned 40. I arranged to have some quiet time in a small Nova Scotia town after my common-law husband left me for a younger woman. I had wanted a child, and was mourning that lost opportunity. The plumbing failed in the small house I was staying in, and I called a local plumber, who was also going through a divorce. Yep—just like in some cheap romance novel, we started this incredible romance (he was quite an interesting and charming person). I got pregnant.
>
> When he learned I was pregnant, he left, and made it clear that he didn't want to be responsible for the baby. In a way, I felt I unconsciously didn't protect myself because I wanted a baby. Anyway, I had her myself, and I guess I had this romantic notion of what having a baby meant. But if someone had warned me how hard it would be, I never would have wanted a baby in the first place! Not that I don't love her with all my heart, but it's difficult, and sometimes an isolating experience at this age.

Do all women ripen?

The short answer is: probably. The ripening process can be a positive or negative experience for women; often there are components of both. Ripening can be a positive awakening that occurs given the appropriate set of circumstances. Women who are living in a state of continuous stress or struggle due to poverty or complete exhaustion, for example, may not experience a positive ripening. These women often shut down and go on a sort of automatic pilot to survive, which is why depression may actually be a sign of ripening gone wrong. The stirrings of this ripening period may be the asking of the "Is this all?" question, but when life seems bleak, and there appear to be no solutions to boredom or lack of challenge, depression may be a way to turn off the inevitable bubbling of passions:

The month before I turned 30 I got pregnant. That was a shock but I was thrilled. Bill got more depressed. He'd come home from work and stare at the TV until he went to bed. I wanted a devoted husband who worked hard and had ambition, and Bill wasn't what I wanted in a husband. I still wanted that storybook ending. It was a big letdown at 30 to finally realize it wasn't going to be. The unhappiness was getting bigger and bigger with Bill, and I was getting more and more tired of it all. By the time the marriage ended it was such a relief...

From 30 to 33 I was happier than when I was married. I was alone, but I was living more on my own terms. I was raising three children. They were my life. My goals were very limited—to survive and raise my kids. I had my own plan to keep sane: I'd be with the kids until they were in school, and then I would go to work. My life was very constricted in those years. I blocked out a lot of feelings, sexuality, everything. I didn't give myself anything to get disappointed in. (Levinson, *The Seasons of a Woman's Life*:136)

THE HISTORY OF RIPENING

Historically, ripening may have been what was going on when women were diagnosed with hysteria (from the Greek word meaning "that which proceeds from the uterus"), a term that remained in the vernacular of medicine from the fourth century B.C. until 1952, when the American Psychiatric Association finally stopped using it. Hysteria was listed as the most common women's disease next to fevers, and was thought to be a disease caused by sexual dissatisfaction (or longing) commonly diagnosed in virgins, young widows and nuns, who were discouraged from the terrible sin of masturbation. Marriage was considered a cure, but clearly, it failed to cure many women. Hysteria was also thought to plague women with more "passionate" natures. In fact, the ancient Greek physician and writer Galen called it a disease of sexual deprivation.

Ripening may have actually created an industry for medical doctors. In her book, *The Technology of Orgasm: Hysteria, the Vibrator, and Women's Sexual Satisfaction*, Rachel P. Maines meticulously documents the standard treatment for hysteria by physicians: manually stimulating the clitoris during the office visit, and bringing the "hysterical" patient to orgasm. This treatment was documented as early as the first century A.D., and continued well into the twentieth century.

Bringing women to orgasm was the bread and butter of many physicians from the time of Hippocrates until the 1920s. In the late nineteenth century, it was documented that 75 percent of the female population required these treatments. Vibrators were invented by physicians as a medical device to save time, since apparently so much of it was spent with patients who came once a week for these treatments.

In short, normal sexual fulfillment became a medical treatment for women. Eventually, the vibrator evolved as a consumer sexual product, putting into the hands of women what Maines says was the "job nobody wanted." Thus, many of the symptoms of sexual dissatisfaction, which characterized hysteria, disappeared as we learned more about the function of the clitoris, and the fact that most women cannot achieve orgasm during intercourse without direct clitoral stimulation.

Ripening or midlife crisis?

Sam Keen, author of *The Passionate Life*, suggests that around midlife, we begin to mourn for our potential: our "unrealized promises haunt." Something urges us to leave the security of personality, position and prestige to venture into the unknown. For women, this often means questioning their long-term relationships. Keen refers to this questioning as the "outlaw quest." We become outlaws in the sense that we begin

to reject the social norms. We enter a period of self-decon-
struction and reconstruction. Keen advises: "If you listen to
the voice of the erotic conscience, it will lead you to the gate-
way of the great liberation."

> Outlaw sexuality is based on the quest for autonomy. What
> do I desire? What are the laws of my own sexuality? For
> most, this stage involves a period of experimentation
> beyond the boundaries of normal sexuality—adultery,
> promiscuity, homosexuality, reversal of normal roles. For
> women, this often means an end to the receptacle theme,
> and a beginning of firmness, focus and aggression.
> Eventually, though, the goal is to free eros from its "genital
> moorings" and imagine a life in which we might be
> connected to the entire environment with the intensity that
> was once reserved for sex. (Keen: 201)

Our personalities may ripen during midlife as well. For
most women, personality is blocked by social roles and
responsibilities. We become, in a sense, addicted to our roles.
We spend our time trying to succeed in terms of career or
beauty, expressed through body image preoccupation, which
consumes our time and energy. We may also become
consumed with acquiring "stuff." In essence, we forget how to
have fun and enjoy ourselves. The desire to burst out, travel,
dance, and so on are an expression of our social role rejection,
and the bursting forth of our repressed personalities.

Gail Sheehy reminds us that the term "midlife" is eroding
since many of us are facing two or three lives by the time we're

40. In my own case, I count my premarried life as one version of life; my married life as a second version of life; and my current, re-singled life as a third version. Anything can happen in my future. I may remarry. I may progress into a series of relationships that could feel like "different lives." The point is that few people have one life anymore, which means that the term "midlife" is no longer appropriate. Where does the middle of one life begin, and the beginning of a new life meet? Sheehy refers to the many lives within our one life as a "disequilibrium." She says: "Three lives in one may sound like a bargain, but it comes at a price."

Ripening as part of the life cycle

Many experts reject the term "midlife crisis" and embrace more accurate terms such as continuous adult learning or adult life cycle.

Daniel Levinson, author of *The Seasons of a Woman's Life*, sees a woman's life cycle as a series of "eras," which his research showed is linked to age, with small bridges between eras he calls "cross-era transitions" that last about five years. For instance, I am in what Levinson calls the Age 30 transition, which began for me at around age 34—right on schedule according to Levinson's research. But my transition is not finished. As of this writing, I am 37, and just a year out of my traditional marriage. Between age 35 and 37 my life went through dramatic, almost unrecognizable changes. I have told friends that I feel as if I'm observing someone else's life. I probably won't be settled into my "new" life until about age 39 or so.

Our early adulthood, according to Levinson, begins around age 17 and lasts until age 45, with our 20s and 30s being peak energy years. Typically, this period is the most stressful time in a woman's life, too. As we age beyond 45, we become more senior members of adulthood, in which love, sexuality, family life, creativity and career can be immensely satisfying:

> Early adulthood is the era in which we are most buffeted by our own passions and ambitions from within, and by the demands of family, community, and society from without. Under reasonably favorable conditions, the rewards of living in this era are enormous; but the costs often equal or exceed the benefits. (Levinson: 20)

Levinson refers to a midlife transition, in which the quality of our lives in the mid 40s is always appreciably different than it was in our late 30s. Some of us may improve our life conditions between our late 30s and mid 40s; some of us may find our lives have either not improved or have become less satisfactory, which is why many of us suffer. The quality of our lives is not measured by financial gain, however, but by spiritual gain. Losing all of our money between age 38 and 45 may help us realize our true potential, for example. Improving our lives has to do with realizing our potential versus preparing for old age. Ripening is a process that takes place within this cross-era transition between early adulthood and later adulthood, as the following anecdote implies:

When I was 32 I'd been on birth control pills for seven years, and the doctor felt I should stop. Kevin got a vasectomy. He warned me at the time that he would then have affairs. I heard him, it registered, but I didn't want to pursue the issue. I guess I could cope with the idea as long as I didn't know about it. We had gone long periods of time without having sex, and I guess I always assumed he was having affairs. At Kevin's urging we started going to a neighbor's house to watch X-rated movies. Then Kevin wanted to swap partners sexually! I refused and stopped going to the neighbor's house, but he continued going there alone.

We were renting part of our house to earn extra income. When I was 32 a young man named Brent moved in, and we became close friends. I learned from him that a person can live alone and take care of themselves and not be dependent on another person to take care of them... I knew I needed to leave the marriage, but I had no place to go and no money...

Kevin gave me permission to have a sexual relationship with Brent. I guess he hoped that would get me more interested in swapping partners with his friends. Brent and I did begin a sexual relationship. It was all so new to me! The only man I had ever slept with was Kevin, and he had been so traditional, so rigid—no oral sex or experimenting. To Brent everything was free, and there were no boundaries. Once I started the sexual relationship with him I realized my marriage was hopeless. I needed to make a life for myself so I could leave the marriage...

I'm 35 now, and for the past year I've worked full time as a typist. I earn less than $10,000 with no support from Kevin. I get food stamps but it's still such a struggle to make ends meet. I plan to marry Brent within the next couple of years and start a new life with him. No matter how difficult it is or what happens in the future, this life is a thousand times better than my marriage was. (Levinson, *The Seasons of a Woman's Life*: 134–35)

RIPENING AND PSYCHOLOGICAL DIVORCE

For many women, the traditional marriage structure is a barrier to freedom, spiritual and sensual awakenings. Thus, one of the most powerful signs of ripening can be seen in the psychological divorcing of a spouse, which is usually more significant to a woman than a legal separation or divorce. Women can live years with a man whom they have psychologically divorced. The severing of the relationship psychologically allows them to seek connection and purpose outside the marriage, and gives them permission to have affairs. In my case, I was married and living with my husband when I moved in with another man. I never considered my actions to be adulterous, for a psychological divorce had already occurred. A year prior, when I merely entertained, but did not act on, a sexual liaison with another man, I felt tremendous guilt, as though I had already committed adultery. The affair in my mind was more of a betrayal prior to my psychological divorce, although to a court, there was no difference legally.

The psychological divorce usually takes place for women sometime in their 30s, when the reality of the marriage structure begins to sink in and women emerge from the fog that clouded their judgment and decisions in their 20s. Sometimes a depression precedes or coincides with this "divorce of the heart. The desire to get married in our 20s is often driven by our yearning for security, stability and normalcy. Once we attain a level of stability, we may find the marriage is lacking a spiritual and emotional dimension.

The most common reasons for a psychological divorce have to do with feelings of abandonment. When women feel as though their spouses are not there on either a concrete or emotional level, they will begin to sever ties. Levinson's research revealed that more women get psychological divorces than legal ones. In fact, the rate of legal divorce, which is bad enough, does not reflect the "unhappiness quotient" so many women endure in traditional marriages. Just because marriages endure doesn't mean they're good marriages. A woman from Levinson's research shares a universal sentiment:

> The marriage had always lacked passion on my part. I have never been fulfilled in my marriage. I have a collection of personal needs that I don't think my husband is capable of meeting or maybe I'm not willing to let him try. There is definitely a holding back on my part as well as a lack of sensitivity on his part. (Levinson, *The Seasons of a Woman's Life*: 246)

Legal divorces usually take place when women have some-where to go. When they have nowhere to go because they have sacrificed their careers for the sake of a traditional marriage structure in which the husband is the income provider, many will divorce in their minds.

Research reveals that exceedingly few women are satisfied within a marriage structure. Levinson's research showed that most women felt they had hit rock bottom by age 40 if they were still married. Almost all of the women Levinson studied felt that their marriages were stagnant, with the husband rarely involved with children and only marginally connected to the wife. Sex was infrequent, most often at the woman's initiative, with her feeling that her husband had little interest in any real personal contact. He seemed only to want his meals cooked, his house cleaned and the appearance of his marriage maintained. Though the women felt totally trapped, many of them still felt that divorce was worse because they had nowhere to go and no means of supporting themselves. One woman Levinson interviewed said: "I feel old at 40. I'm utterly isolated and alone and used up. There is no love in my life. I'm too young to live like this. It's as though I'm in the middle of a dark hole and there is no way out. I can't go on like this much longer." (Levinson: 174)

Although this woman's statement sounds far from ripening, it is, in fact, the first sign of it. She is starting to awaken, and to see that she is surely too young to feel so old. When women feel this sort of reality within, the eventual move is away from their marriage to start exploring other ways to live. As women start to desire more, the ripening process is initiated. Often, however, women seek out negative experiences in a quest for satisfying their desires; women may not only wander into painful affairs, but into addictions. Cocaine addiction, for example, is a common addiction in 30-something and 40-something women because the sensation of cocaine is thrilling. Many women find it is the first pleasure that is just for them.

A typical story of the psychologically divorced woman comes from Levinson's research:

> In my late thirties I began to look at my marriage. I was taking care of him and the children and everyone and everything else, and so someone was supposed to be making me happy. My husband was a workaholic and had always been emotionally distant from the children and me. He was quite alcoholic. There was almost nothing between us. He'd come home, we'd have a silent dinner, and we'd each go our separate ways. He'd go to bed first and be asleep by the time I'd go to bed. If I got to bed early, he'd stay up until he was sure I was asleep. We only had sex a couple of times a year, always at my initiative. He had premature ejaculation, and there was never any holding or feeling that he really wanted to make love with me. He was so withholding; he gave me very little. He seemed totally happy with the arrangement—and why not? He got some-one to cook his meals, keep his house clean and do the laundry. I felt totally trapped. I felt I couldn't divorce because I had no place to go, no job, no money. I got very depressed. I was in my late thirties, in a loveless, sexless

marriage, and felt like an old woman who had been used up and thrown away...

And now, we clearly see this woman's ripening:

Returning to college saved my life and gave me hope for the future. I was in a wonderful world of ideas and study, and I made wonderful friendships with other women my age who had gone back to school too. It was the best time of my life, and I never wanted it to end. Going to college helped me to stay in my marriage and earn a credential that would allow me to earn a living for myself and my children if I decided to leave the marriage. It also took my mind off my terrible marriage and gave me a whole new world full of interesting people who found me interesting.

As graduation approached, the marriage became intolerable. I decided, "I can't live like this anymore; I have no life. What do I get out of this marriage? Am I supposed to have a sexless marriage or am I supposed to go out and have affairs? We live together but there is very little between us, and it has become intolerable.

The pain of the divorce was almost unbearable. The pain came from the fragmentation of my life, the loss of the matrix in which I had lived for all those years, the sense of aloneness, the awareness of how much growing up I had to do in order to establish a better life. (Levinson, *The Seasons of a Woman's Life*: 190–91)

REALIZATION OF THE TRADE

Passions stir, and the ripening process begins when women realize they've made a trade. What I call the "Trade," Valerie Gibson, relationship guru for the *Toronto Sun*, calls the "Deal." Almost without exception, women will trade passion for security when they choose a marriage partner. Even financially secure, educated women will make this trade for the emotional security they get. Statistically, far more female graduate students do not finish their degrees, or do not pursue their careers after obtaining their degrees.

A woman from Levinson's research tells this universal8story:

> In looking for a marriage partner, I was companionship-oriented and willing to scrap a lot of other things for a person who would be a good friend, which Carl clearly was. What I left out in that rational equation was sex. Ultimately that was a pretty serious mistake because sex never really clicked between us. The whole relationship was founded on companionship. I thought of Carl as protective, strong, and capable. I had found someone, instead of my father, who would look after me, protect me, and let me do my own thing. That's what I needed most at the time.
>
> The sexual part was not overly passionate. If the person you share your life with is a good steady friend and companion, I figured then sex will work out reasonably well. It's not the most important thing in the world. But sex never did work

out reasonably well for us. It was tolerable for a brief time. We had not been totally intimate before marriage, and it was a total disaster when we started. It took a long time to recover from that. (Levinson, *The Seasons of a Woman's Life*: 246–47)

Another woman shares her Trade:

That spring I decided to apply to a different graduate school. At about the same time Jay proposed marriage. I didn't feel especially happy about marrying him. Our relationship was not passionate. It certainly wasn't the optimal circumstances under which to make that kind of commitment; it was really a way of being safe again. Marrying Jay seemed like the right thing to do, but it wasn't as joyful as it should have been, and I certainly recognized that at the time. On the day I got married I did not feel especially happy.

We married that summer, when I was 23. We had applied to the same universities, and in the fall we both went to the same one but in different departments. Once again, I made a choice based in *his* preference. That was the beginning of a relatively stable but not exciting time. We had our own separate worlds and friends. We didn't fight, but we didn't have much of a relationship either. Though I enjoyed graduate school and did well enough, I still didn't know where it was leading. (Levinson, *The Seasons of a Woman's Life*, 253)

Studies show that, alas, very few educated, career-driven women actually marry for love. They marry for affection and support, but not passion or sexual interest. Most women grow to become sexually dissatisfied as they age in their marriages, and most are surprised by how uneven the sharing of parenting and household tasks become. In most cases, it is the woman who initiates the divorce, either psychologically or legally, and in studies, 50 percent of married women with careers will begin affairs sometime in their 30s, although in some cases, with the husband's knowledge through an open marriage (something my husband and I actually discussed but dismissed).

The majority of women who make the Trade are not passionately connected with their spouses. As the years pass, the loneliness drives most of them into a sexual awakening, where they seek out passionate sex or intimacy through affairs.

> *Ripening is many things: it is a time of questioning, deconstructing, reconstructing and, for many married women, realizing that marriage, for the most part, benefits the man and not the woman.*
>
> *Marriage as an institution tends to protect men from depression, leaving women vulnerable to it, because within the structure of traditional marriage, where women raise the children and men earn the income, men spend more time outside the structure than women, who become tied to, if not trapped, within it. Even in the modified structure, where women work and*

raise the children, they are still left unfulfilled—but more tired. Happy marriages are far less common than ailing marriages because of the Trade. Thus, within the process of ripening, a depression can emerge. When there is no opportunity for their passions to be realized, women will shut down, turn off and emerge into a flatness, discussed next.

3

THE ABSENCE
OF PASSION
DEPRESSION

When there is an absence of passion, our lives become flat and featureless. This is known as depression, which is not so much characterized by sadness as by a numbness or lack of engagement in life.

Depression is accompanied by a loss of interest and pleasure in once-enjoyable activities. For women, most social and situational triggers of depression are linked to an absence of passion. One of the most significant causes for an absence of passion is the absence of a sexually satisfying relationship, which also contributes to feelings of low self-esteem. Women who make the Trade, for example, are prone to depression at some point in their marriage. But there are a range of social situations that exist for women which can trigger depression. This chapter will help you understand depression as a normal response to an absence of passion in our lives.

WHEN WE STOP
"FEELING OUR LIVES"

Passion was defined earlier as "feeling our lives" or feeling our mortality. Hence, anything that involves feelings, even negative feelings, such as sadness or anger, are still expressions of passion. Both anger and sadness, for example, are mobilizing; depression is immobilizing. Danish philosopher Søren Kierkegaard believed that a person who never knows melancholy will never know metamorphosis either. Thus, feelings of tremendous sadness or grief are important aspects of the human condition. When these feelings are repressed, there are consequences.

Depression is distinct from sadness in that it is usually a point beyond it, characterized by a numbness and inability to act or communicate. Some researchers suggest that the inability to act or communicate has a larger purpose for people at the crossroads in life. When you find your values and goals are shifting, or stirring, and you're in a state of confusion, often the worst thing you can do is act or make a decision. That period of indecision is valuable for it enables you to stop and reflect. This is why depression may be the first sign of a ripening.

Angst, a feature of depression, was described by Kierkegaard as a sign that one is realizing the field of possibilities that comes from free will. It is a time when we are contemplating our past choices or circumstances and thinking about ways to make new choices or change circumstances. The philosopher Martin Heidegger discussed anxiety, which often accompanies depression, as an indication that the world (situations, relationships, contacts) isn't "working" for us anymore, forcing us to reconstruct the world around us. This is what many of the women's stories in chapter 2 confirmed.

When we are faced with challenging an old way of being or thinking, many of us enter depression in order to deal with the crisis and hopefully emerge more true to ourselves. Whether depression entails a slowing down, or a complete halt, these symptoms may be necessary in order for us to do an emotional map of rerouting and changing direction emotionally so that we can either continue along the road to self-actualization, or perhaps discover it for the first time.

Self-actualization may or may not lead to greater happiness or fulfillment, however, for indeed, ignorance is still bliss. Indeed, greater self-knowledge tends to burst bubbles and tears down walls we've spent years erecting to protect ourselves. Unfortunately, human beings are driven to the path that leads to greater truth. Whether the truth is forced upon us through circumstances beyond our control, or we (un)consciously set ourselves up to discover it, truth is like a birth: it is born out of pain and suffering. Sometimes, when the pain and suffering is too great, we give ourselves an emotional epidural that numbs things for a while, which manifests as a depression. Polly hadn't realized how numb she was until she saw herself captured on video, at her son's seventh birthday party:

> I had been feeling very blah, which seemed to start some-time after my son was born, but just never went away. I thought this was how life was just supposed to be... routine, mundane. Every decision started to feel like too much—even about which bread or ice cream to buy. Since I had

left my job to take care of my son, I guess I never noticed how out of it I was. Then I saw the birthday video my husband took of our son's party. For a couple of seconds, I saw a stranger in the video I don't remember inviting, who was wearing my dress. She looked completely drained of life and energy, which is why I didn't notice at first that the woman was me. When I realized I was seeing myself, I turned off the video at once. Later that night, I spent hours in the basement, digging out pictures of myself from a time forgotten... when I was alive. That was a turning point for me, and I sought out a really good therapist. At first I was in denial about how dreary my life had become, but when I realized that my husband hadn't even kissed me in over three years, the haze over my life started to clear. I was lonely and I had just shut down.

Signs of depression

Depression is clinically known as a mood disorder. It's impossible to define what a "normal mood" is since we have complex personalities and exhibit different moods throughout a given week, or even a given day. However, it's not impossible for you to define what a "normal" mood is for *you*. You know how you feel when you're functional: you're eating, sleeping, interacting with friends and family, being productive, active and generally interested in daily goings-on. Well, depression occurs when you feel you've lost the ability to function for a prolonged period of time, or if you're functioning at a reasonable level to the outside world, you've lost interest in participating in life.

One bad day, or even a bad week (which will usually be made up of some relief time when you can laugh at something or take pleasure in something) from time to time, is not a sign that you're depressed. Feeling you've lost the ability to function as you normally do, all day, every day, for a period of at least two weeks, may be a sign that you're depressed. The symptoms of depression vary from person to person, but can include some or all of the following:

- Feelings of sadness and/or empty mood;

- Difficulty sleeping (usually waking up frequently in the middle of the night);

- Loss of energy and feelings of fatigue and lethargy;

- Change in appetite (usually a loss of appetite);

- Difficulty thinking, concentrating or making decisions;

- Loss of interest in formerly pleasurable activities, including sex;

- Anxiety or panic attacks;

- Obsessing over negative experiences or thoughts;

- Feeling guilty, worthless, hopeless or helpless;

- Feeling restless and irritable; and

- Thinking about death or suicide.

Maria shares her memories of depression:

It's hard to explain what it's like to spend six weeks in bed... I was not so much tired, but tired of my life. I did not have the will to get out of bed to answer the phone or check my e-mail. Eventually, I just unplugged the phone so the ringing would stop. Part of me wanted to get back, but I couldn't find that missing piece of myself to get back. My sleep wasn't sleep but just closing my eyes and hoping to fade away. But then the pounding would start; the thought of getting up and facing people would make my heart pound and my head spin, and I couldn't catch my breath. If I put my pillow over my head, I could make the pounding stop.

This went on for weeks. My sister had a key to my apartment. One day she just came into my room and literally dragged me out of bed. She had bought all kinds of breakfast foods. But when I got up it was dark—it was nighttime. She said: "For you, it's morning, so we're having breakfast." She wanted to take me to the hospital, but I wouldn't go. After what seemed like an eternity of arguing (I kept wanting to go back to bed), I agreed to go to Loblaws with her the next day and stock my fridge. That was the beginning of the "lift"—and my thirty-ninth year. I was so afraid of turning 40 and feeling old, and still being alone, I guess I turned off my feelings for a while.

When you can't sleep

The typical sleep pattern of a depressed person is to go to bed at the normal time, only to wake up around two in the morning, and find that she can't get back to sleep. The sleepless person spends endless hours watching infomercials to pass the time, lies in bed tossing and turning, usually obsessing over negative experiences or thoughts. Lack of sleep affects the ability to function, and leads to increased irritability, lack of energy and fatigue. Insomnia, by itself, is not a sign of depression, but when you look at depression as a package of symptoms, the inability to fall or stay asleep can aggravate all your other symptoms. In some cases, people who are depressed will oversleep, requiring 10 to 12 hours of sleep every night.

When you can't think clearly

Another debilitating feature of depression is finding that you can't concentrate or think clearly. You feel scattered, disorganized and unable to prioritize. This usually hits hardest in the workplace or in a centre of learning, and can severely impair performance on the job. You may miss important deadlines, important meetings, or find you can't focus when you do go to meetings. When you can't think clearly, you can be overwhelmed with feelings of helplessness or hopelessness. "I can't even perform a simple task such as X anymore" may dominate your thoughts, while you become more disillusioned with your dwindling productivity.

Anna was a copywriter in a busy advertising agency and recalls her own struggles with not being able to think clearly:

> I was in the midst of a very stressful ad campaign and needed to work up new copy for a presentation the next day. Normally, I would take my laptop home, take a bath, and the creativity would just come. I was considered to be

the creative genius at my agency. I had been feeling sort of all over the place and wasn't really myself, but didn't realize how bad it was until I couldn't clear my head when I was soaking in my tub. That night, I took six baths, hoping that the juices would come back.

At 2:00 a.m., when I still had nothing, I started to get out of the tub and then felt my heart racing and sinking all at once. I couldn't breathe, and just sat down and tried to calm myself by splashing cold water on my face from the tub faucet. I called a freelancer I knew, left an urgent message and subbed out the project, paying him out of my own pocket.

Things just got worse at work, and I felt as though I had lost the ability to think. In the end, everything was a mess, and I left my job. Then I left my boyfriend. Then I left my apartment. Everyone said I had burnout. The truth is, I was tired of the constant stress of that job, the nowheresville of my commitment-phobic, toxic boyfriend and my mouse-infested apartment.

A word about anxiety

The anxiety or panic attacks women experience along with their sense of flatness or emptiness is a common characteristic in depression. It is my own theory (which is not based on science or a formal study) that the "pounding" or panic attack is a glimpse of the passions trying to break through the cloud of depression. When we are depressed, we are numb; we are not feeling. The panic is a sort of rush of feeling that hits us—like a repressed memory. If we look at the story of the woman in bed for six weeks, and the one who took six baths in one night, the descriptions of their panic attacks are similar. In the bedridden woman's case, the panic hit her when she contemplated emerging from bed; in the bathing woman's case, the panic hit her when she, in fact, emerged from the tub. Why? The bed and tub were both safe places the women went when they felt overwhelmed by the external world. Leaving their safety and going out into the real world created a fear of feeling, hence facing, their lives, which in an absence of feeling is too much feeling to handle at once.

In chapter 2, I discuss my own story of having fled my marriage. Emerging from my own flatness, I recall crumbling to the floor of the small apartment to which I felt my life had been reduced. Throughout my marriage I feared this fate, and actually had panic attacks when I imagined having to leave my house for a depressing apartment; I stayed in my marriage longer than I should have because I thought I could not survive this experience and did not want to give up my house. When it actually occurred, and I was crouched on that horrible kitchen floor, sobbing, a single thought kept threading in my head: "At least I'm feeling now... at least I'm feeling now..." I cried every night for the first month I was there. Slowly, as I felt again, and ultimately, *felt my life*, I understood what my panic attacks were about: *avoiding* facing and feeling my life. I believe that this is the case for many women struggling with depression, as Celia validates:

I realized I had married the wrong man the day of our wedding. I felt he was wrong. But I couldn't admit it to myself. When my daughter was 4 and my son was 2, everything inside me started to crack. I had terrible panic attacks and my doctor put me on medication that didn't help. I just couldn't function and was almost paralyzed by these anxiety attacks, which were coming on strong... two or three times a day. A girlfriend I confided in pleaded with me to call her therapist who she said was very good with women in bad marriages. I went to see this woman, and she changed my life. She told me I was having anxiety because I knew I had to make a difficult decision—a decision I was dreading because I loved my children and didn't want them to be in a broken home. Eventually, I did make the choice, and my husband agreed to move out. I felt immediate relief when he left. My panic vanished, and I appreciated so much the value of just living again without the anxiety.

Anhedonia: When nothing gives you pleasure

One of the most telling signs of depression is a loss of interest in activities that used to excite you or give you pleasure. This is known as anhedonia, derived from the word "hedonism" (meaning the "philosophy of pleasure"); a hedonist is a person who indulges every pleasure without considering (or caring about) the consequences. Anhedonia simply means "no pleasure."

Different people have different ways of expressing anhedonia. You might tell your friends, for example, that you don't "have any desire" to do X or Y; you can't "get motivated"; or X or Y just doesn't "hold your interest or attention." You may also notice that the sense of satisfaction from a job well done is gone, which is particularly debilitating in the workplace or in a place of learning. For example, artists (photographers, painters, writers) may find the passion has gone out of their work.

Many of the other symptoms of depression hinge on this loss of pleasure. One of the reasons weight loss is so common in depression (typically, people may notice as much as a 10-pound drop in weight) is that food no longer gives them pleasure, or cooking no longer gives them pleasure. The sense of satisfaction we get from having a clean home or clean kitchen may also disappear. Therefore, tackling cleaning up the kitchen in order to prepare food may be too taxing, contributing to a lack of interest in food.

Of course, gaining weight is also not unusual: 10 pounds in the opposite direction can occur, too. This is often due to poor nutrition as well. We fill up on snack foods, or high-calorie, low-nutrient foods because we're not motivated to prepare or eat well-balanced meals. Weight gain may also come from a loss of interest in physical activities—exercising, sports or a dozen other things that keep us active when we're feeling "ourselves."

A loss of interest in sex aggravates matters if we are in a sexual relationship with someone. Again, the decreased desire for sex stems from general anhedonia. Sally recalls:

I was preparing for my first show of watercolours... or should I say, *not* preparing. I had not painted for more than two years, and all of my work was in storage. All I was required to do was get the paintings, organize them in some sort of thematic way and deliver them to the gallery. But I couldn't. The gallery finally arranged for someone else to get them, and asked me to be on hand as they were hung and displayed.

I looked at the paintings, which used to mean everything to me and felt nothing. The colours seemed flat... all wrong. It was as though someone else had painted them. A part of me thought I might feel like painting again if only I could appreciate the work. But there was just emptiness. I had never lost interest in my own work before like this. I knew then that something was terribly wrong and called a dear friend who lived in England. We had gone to art college together, and hearing her voice made me feel, for a moment, like myself.

The day the show opened, I left for England and stayed with my friend for two months. I couldn't care less about the show, and didn't even tell the gallery that I was leaving. When they couldn't get in touch with me, they were kind enough to store my work. All I knew was that I needed to be somewhere that reminded me of my old self—the self that had hope and promise, who had not given up.

WHAT CAUSES DEPRESSION?

Since most episodes of depression are triggered by life events or circumstances, the causes of depression are different for everyone. In a very general way, the direct answer to "who gets depressed?" is: people living in difficult circumstances. Understanding what's "difficult" is akin to understanding pain thresholds. What one woman finds difficult, another may not.

Experts in feminist therapy assert that depression may be a normal state of being for women in our society. These sentiments are echoed by the work of Phyllis Chesler, author of the groundbreaking *Women and Madness*, published in 1972. Chesler exposed the so-called symptoms of depression as simply *healthy* responses to a sick role women were playing in society.

Chesler describes the first European madhouses as nothing short of prisons for the wives and daughters of men. As early as the sixteenth century, wives were thrown into madhouses or royal towers by their husbands as punishment for not conforming or behaving. Soon, private madhouses came into vogue, which were for-profit institutions designed as drop-off centres for rich husbands to dump their wives. Chesler tracks the history of psychiatric imprisonment throughout the centuries, and points out that until the 1970s, the majority of women in mental hospitals were committed involuntarily, or while they were in a coma, following an unsuccessful suicide attempt.

Chesler also observes that the players in the drama of mental hospital "scenes" mimic the witchcraft trials. The male doctors star as the "Inquisitors"; a subservient female nurse stars as the "Handmaiden," while a female patient stars as a "Witch," possessed by unhappiness, powerlessness and dependence. These images still pervade mental health. In a 1998 article on depression, the visual accompanying the article was that of a woman lying on a hospital bed, with wires attached to her head and a plastic device inside her mouth. Around her hovered male doctors in white lab coats, with beards and glasses. The article was discussing brain research and the differences between male and female brain responses to cortisol, a hormone produced by the body while under stress.

By the twentieth century, Chesler asserts, male psychiatrists were acting as agents for husbands unhappy with their wives. This differed from the seventeenth century in that the husbands now appeared to be innocent bystanders while the psychiatrists recommended institutionalization. By 1964, the number of American women seeking psychiatric services climbed to unprecedented heights, and adult female patients exceeded the number of adult male patients. As of 1992, women accounted for roughly two-thirds of psychiatric consumers; 84 percent of all psychotherapy patients were reportedly women, while out of all new patients in psychotherapy each year, 60 percent were reportedly women.

Chesler uses the term "career psychiatric patients," or long-term psychiatric patients—mostly women—which began to emerge in Western culture between 1950 and 1970. During this period, Chesler notes, not only were more women suffering "nervous breakdowns" than men, but curiously, more married women suffered from psychiatric diseases than single women, suggesting that a silencing of women's autonomy was a major contributor. Chesler also suggests that the symptoms that comprise depression in the DSM–IV (*Diagnostic and Statistical Manual of Mental Disorders, 4th Edition*) are, in fact, feminine behaviours that were adopted to survive under oppressive sexist conditions. In essence: real oppression of women caused real distress and unhappiness.

THE CAREER PSYCH PATIENT

The phenomenon of the career or long-term psychiatric patient emerged in Western culture between 1950 and 1970. As mentioned above, not only were more women suffering nervous breakdowns than men, more married women suffered from psychiatric diseases than single women. Feminist scholars also note the following:

- There was limited social tolerance for women who behaved differently than what was expected within their social roles (and hence, they were judged to be neurotic or psychotic). That is, women were frequently perceived as "sick" when they rejected the female role (and frequently, when she accepts the role, and adopts passive behaviour, she is also told she is "sick").

- Women in urban North America (which favoured the nuclear family over the extended family) who outlived their husbands, and who reached menopause, were left "unemployed" at an early age. With the extended family shrinking after the Second World War, they were left without a family to rear; there was no role for women.

- Women tend to seek help more often than men, and
  tend to report their distress more willingly than men.

These three factors helped mobilize women into psychiatrist's offices to seek help for feeling "not fulfilled" with the
role of wife and mother.

Some depressing circumstances

It's useful to look at the life events that are common triggers
of situational depression in women. Many of the symptoms of
depression are understandable and logical, given some of the
following situations. In other words, you'd be crazy not to
be depressed!

Keep in mind that the following list is certainly not exhaus-
tive, but is designed to give you a general scope of women's
experiences. (I've left birthdays off the list, but they are
frequent triggers of depressive episodes because they repre-
sent aging, feelings of loss of beauty, vitality and power.)

- *Violence.* One of the most identifiable difficult circumstances is violence, which is discussed in detail in
  chapter 5.

- *Poverty.* Single women and women of colour are far
  more likely to live in poverty than white men. After a
  divorce, a man's income increases by roughly 20
  percent, yet a women's income decreases by at least 50
  percent. In 1995, the average income for a Canadian
  male was $40,419, compared to just $27,624 for a

Canadian woman. Difficulty paying bills and making ends meet leads to feelings of anxiousness, sleeplessness, stress, guilt, irritability and persistent physical symptoms. And poverty is tiring: many women need to work at two or three jobs in order to survive, and cannot afford some of the conveniences that make life easier. This can lead to fatigue, loss of energy and loss of appetite, among other things.

Women in debt is a new spin on poverty; the poverty is often hidden by women who are living in seemingly comfortable surroundings, even though they have maxed out their credit cards to pay the rent in between jobs or contracts; are being harassed by creditors; and are one day away from having their car repossessed. That said, spending beyond one's means is often a sign of mania, discussed in the next chapter.

It's also important to note that many women in poverty or debt are also the hidden homeless. Untold numbers of women camp out on the couches of friends and relatives while looking for employment or a place to live.

- *Workplace stress and/or harassment.* Even though it's the twenty-first century, women still must cope with sexual harassment, ageism and sexism in the workplace, which often leads to loss of employment. Those women forced to work two jobs to make ends meet can be exposed to twice the abuse on the job in the form of harassment or stress. As well, plain old stress caused by the long hours and commuting all people in the workplace endure can also trigger depression.

- *Beauty standards.* Impossible standards of beauty are another factor that makes life difficult for women. Aside from body image anxiety, the physical symptoms caused by any resulting eating disorders can cause restlessness, irritability, difficulty concentrating or making decisions, loss of interest in formerly pleasurable activities, feelings of self-doubt and self-hatred.

- *Hormonal factors.* Hormonal changes related to the menstrual cycle, pregnancy, postpartum changes and menopause could certainly be looked upon as organic causes of depression, in that hormones can alter behaviour and moods, but many women argue that there are social stigmas attached to menstruation and menopause, too, which cannot be ignored. Heavy, crampy periods (often a sign of endometriosis) or an unexpected period (due to the unpredictability of menopausal changes) in the middle of a busy workday is not an insignificant stress. Menopause is a social symbol of aging in Western culture, which has a number of powerful feelings associated with it.

- *Illness.* A related factor in many cases of depression is chronic illness. Women living with arthritis, osteoporosis, colitis, HIV-AIDS, cancer and other chronic diseases frequently experience many of the symptoms associated with depression, such as loss of appetite, sleeplessness and loss of interest in formerly pleasurable activities. To aggravate matters, medications, used in a variety of situations, ranging from chemotherapy to AZT, can also cause depression.

- *Infertility.* Roughly 20 percent of Canadian couples are infertile. A study by Harvard professor Dr. Alice Domar found that women who were undergoing fertility treatment experienced levels of depression that equalled those of women facing cancer or AIDS. First, the circumstance of infertility, by itself, can trigger all the feelings and symptoms associated with biological depression. Meanwhile, the hormonal changes created by fertility drugs can also trigger biological depression; estrogen functions as a weak antidepressant, and when fertility drugs are introduced, mood can head south. Then, the cost of treatment can place a strain on finances, which adds to depression. There is also grief involved with being labelled infertile, as women tend to mourn for their unborn children, and must accept a change in identity from mother-to-be to childless woman.

- *Pregnancy loss.* This is a common trigger for depression in women of childbearing age. One in six pregnancies ends in miscarriage, but as women age, the miscarriage rate increases. Women who have struggled with infertility also miscarry at higher rates.

- *Divorce.* Whether you were living common-law or were married, the dissolution of a long-term relationship with an intimate partner leads to feelings of grief, sadness, loneliness, isolation and often financial hardship: all fodder for a depressive episode.

- *Ailing marriage.* As discussed in chapter 2, living in an ailing, passionless marriage (common-law or legal) can also be a trigger for depression.

HOW TO FEEL AGAIN

There is no one way to stop the suffering in depression. Different things work for different women. Because women suffer more when they are feeling disconnected, finding someone to talk to in the form of a counsellor or support group is a good way to begin to feel again. There are also a number of self-healing strategies that can accompany talk therapy, which I prefer to call "seeking connection."

When women seek connection with other women, some of the things they talk about might include:

1. *Sexism.* In case you haven't noticed, we live in a sexist society where men still enjoy more privileges than women. Ask other women how they feel about that. Your conversation won't change the world, but your feelings about the world might be validated. And that feels good.

2. *Powerlessness.* You know what? You feel powerless because you're set up to feel powerless—by those in power! Most women have very little power in their workplace, home or community. So it's no wonder you feel inadequate. Talking about this may help you find a perspective that actually empowers you. By the way, this is not to say that there are no powerful women in the world; it's just that they are few and far between. And there are plenty of women in power who feel powerless, too.

4. *Ambivalence over assertiveness.* I know it's the twenty-first century, but women in many cultures are still

taught to be docile and passive in a world that is aggressive and harsh. Again, talking about it won't necessarily change you into a go-getter, but it will probably help you realize that you're not the only one out there who has been taught to feel that assertiveness is unfeminine. Therefore, your reluctance to assert yourself is perfectly understandable, given the message you're sent from birth: you do not have a voice and when you speak, negative consequences follow.

5. *Absurd standards of beauty.* Spend an afternoon with a fashion photographer and makeup artist, and they can tell you quite a few things. For example, what you see in magazines is fiction and fantasy with the aid of heavy makeup, carefully constructed lighting and computer-aided touch-ups. In fact, it's common for fashion models to self-induce vomiting prior to a photo shoot (the makeup artists can smell the vomit on the model while she's in makeup). Is that beautiful? Talk about *that* with other women!

One makeup artist put it best when he told me: "I can't even watch television or read a magazine anymore because I know how ugly this business is, and how desperate the women are who participate in this sham. We [makeup artists and photographers] spend hours distorting these women and dare call it 'beauty.'"

When it is the Caucasian face that is objectified and held up as the global standard of beauty, what are you supposed to do if you're not Caucasian? Does this standard of beauty make sense to you? And when 17-year-old girls are objectified and held up as the standard for what a 35-year-old woman is supposed to look like, isn't that insane? Tall women are considered more beautiful than Caucasian women of average height. So if you're of average height for a Caucasian, you're not considered beautiful enough for the Western standard. But of course, most women on the planet are not Caucasian. The average height for Asian women, for example, is shorter than the average Caucasian height. Clearly, our beauty standards are not sane.

The message of seeking comfort in validation is not to confirm your suspicions that life is horrible and hopeless but that you're not the only one who feels life is a struggle. This should give you the courage to move forward and make some changes (or at least, make some friends who have common concerns) instead of shrinking in a corner feeling you're the only one.

The sharing approach has been shown to be highly beneficial, particularly in cases where women share difficult circumstances or have difficulties in common. Professionals who provide counselling for women report that the support and confidence gained from other women, including woman-centred counselling, is very helpful.

This isn't just true for depression. Several studies have shown the value of support groups and support systems in treating many physical diseases, such as cancer. One study found that women with end-stage breast cancer who joined a support group actually lived longer than women who did not seek support. And women who share common conditions, such as infertility, AIDS and pregnancy, find support groups enormously helpful.

Since depression has so many causes, support groups for depressed women are not as useful as support groups for, say, women who are living with violence, or women who are battling obesity. In other words, finding or establishing a group of women who share your *circumstances* is the key to finding good support. Otherwise, you may wind up in a group where your circumstances are not understood at all. For example, if you were going through a divorce, someone coping with cancer may find your circumstances not reason enough for you to feel depressed. Or, someone with AIDS may find someone with a treatable cancer unreasonable in her feelings of depression.

Community and cultural norms are also a huge factor in finding the right support group. For example, East Indian women may cope differently than Asian women, while African-American women may cope differently than Caribbean or Somali women.

Where do you look for support? If you're struggling with making ends meet you won't likely find an ad in the paper inviting "All Poor Women" to a support group. But if you live in a poor community, responding to community-based programs, ranging from crafts groups to yoga, is the way to support. In fact, community outreach workers use the arts, crafts, fitness, computer classes and so on as a tool to attract women within the community who could benefit from support. What often takes place in community-based programs is a great deal of talking and sharing during, prior to or after the activity. These are places where you make friends; find someone you can talk to; and most importantly, find that you're not alone in your situation. Community programs are a way for women to say to their abusive husbands: "Back in an hour; I'm going to my yoga class," instead of: "I'm going to talk about what a bastard you are to a bunch of other women living with bastards!"

The old joke about women going to the bathroom in twos is quite accurate; women go together to the bathroom because it's a place where they can talk. Women *need* other women to talk to. This is how we've been coping with the hardships of life for centuries. One study found that women have an average of about 4 to 6 close friendships with other women; men average 0 to 1 close friendship with another male.

Myra shares her healing experience of connecting with other women in her circumstances:

> I was in pretty bad shape when I joined Weight Watchers, and had sort of tuned out the world at that time. I didn't expect to find therapy but I did. I started to live for my meetings. I actually didn't lose as much weight as I had hoped, but I did gain some really good friends. We all had similar struggles. In my case, my husband started to badger me about my weight after I had a baby. I just couldn't lose the weight. Everytime he commented to me about "joining a gym" or something like that, I would go into our walk-in closet and start crying, claiming I was looking for a particular shoe or something. Eventually I just started to feel nothing at all. But when I listened to the weight struggle stories of other women in my group, whose boyfriends or husbands

were also commenting about their weight, I didn't feel as isolated. I saw the problem as something we all shared rather than my own.

WOMEN-CENTRED THERAPY

Countless studies have shown that freedom from oppressive marriages, relationships, careers/workplaces or parents, freedom to act as adults and make their own choices can do amazing things for women's self-esteem and help them rediscover their passions from within. A woman-centred approach to therapy means looking at ways, with your therapist, to liberate yourself from situations that undermine your freedom to make your own decisions, or rob you of your self-esteem and self-worth, and passion for life. A woman-centred approach to therapy helps women:

1.   develop a sense of self, independent of male authority or idealized visions of what a woman is supposed to be; the task is not for a woman to develop a male persona but to celebrate her own feminine persona and to see her traits as inner strength rather than an inability to compete in a male world.

2.   see that the "personal is political," as the adage goes. Feminist therapists listen for the connections between the personal story and the outer world in women's lives. The therapist uses feminist values to help shift women from a victim into a person who sees how the

world around her creates her feelings of victimization—
which is therefore validating.

3. see that depression is really the internalization of
oppression. (This does not mean, however, that you
should just walk around depressed and not seek help!)

4. see that their feelings of low self-esteem, worthless-
ness, inadequacy, powerlessness, poor body image,
anxiety, depression and/or sexual dysfunction are symptoms of female subservience in a man's world. In other
words, they are normal, adaptive responses to the world
around them, rather than symptoms of a disease or sick-
ness. (Again, this does not mean that you should shrug
off your feelings of depression, low self-esteem and so
on, and not get help.

5. see that their self-sacrificing behaviours are normal
feminine, nurturing behaviours rather than symptoms of a
disease. Labels such as "co-dependent" are not helpful,
and should be dismissed as psychobabble.

6. see that their physical ailments are valid and should
be trusted as another way of "knowing." In other words,
women's bodies may be trying to tell them something
about the environment or the toxic lifestyle to which we
have become numb.

7. understand that their psyche exists within the society
or the social relationships that surround it.

8. understand that their behaviour in therapy is intricately connected to their therapist. For example, many women who in the past saw male therapists who were patriarchal in their approaches acted out "father-daughter" dramas in their therapy instead of becoming more empowered in their lives.

9. see that human emotional pain is not a medical problem but a normal response to one's environment. In other words, pain in response to a bad situation is normal, not sick.

10. understand that grief is grief. Grieving over the death of a loved one is not different from grieving over one's poverty or life circumstances. Yet, in the medical world, some things are more worthy of grief than others, meaning that you are labelled normal for some kinds of grieving but sick for other kinds.

11. connect to other women as a group. What you suffer, other women suffer. You are not alone, but part of a community. The solution cannot be found on an individual level, but must be arrived at collectively. In other words, one African-American person in 1950 could not overturn centuries of racism and segregation. It took a movement, not one person.

In this chapter, I discuss depression from the perspective of the absence of passion, and examine the value of reconnection as a way of feeling again, as well as seeking woman-centred talk therapy. These are perspectives you will find largely absent from current books about depression. That said, this chapter does not cover the extensive literature on types of depression, and other forms of treatment, including the various styles of talk therapy (such as cognitive therapy), or the role of medication, herbal remedies and lifestyle changes, such as diet and exercise. For a more extensive view of depression from both a sociological and clinical perspective, see my book Women and Sadness: A Sane Approach To Depression. *The next chapter explores what Freud called a defence against depression: mania.*

4

PASSIONATE RESCUE
MANIA

When I began to think about passion and the stories of women I knew or interviewed who suffered from manic depression (now called bipolar disorder), I developed a theory that I felt was validated by a statement made by Sigmund Freud: mania is a defence against depression. That is, mania, which is "pure passion" (as you'll see from the list of symptoms further on, which come from the DSM–IV) may be a defence against the societal structures in place that threaten to rob us of our passions and creativity. For women, these include the social role structures of wife and mother.

Countless gifted, brilliant women suffered from manic depression, including Virginia Woolf, Sylvia Plath and Anne Sexton. Some of the most beautiful, inspired creative work often emerges through mania, while there is a large body of literature about creativity and mania. The state of mania or euphoria often drives creativity, while creativity fuels the mania.

When looking at creative women from the not-too-distant past, it is clear that their manic states offered rescue from their social roles. Mania induces many "male" feelings: power; sexual potency; aggressiveness; feelings of grandeur; tremendous confidence and ego. These are feelings that few women ever experience. The manic woman pays for these feelings with a "crash," as we'll explore. It can be argued, however, that the cost is worth it for women who would otherwise find life without passion and creativity intolerable.

Please take the information in this chapter as my own artistic expression, which I present to you as a free thinker, not as a scientist. You will be hard-pressed to find a practising mental health expert who agrees with my theory about mania, and were this a book intended as a practical guide to mental health, I would withhold information that was not scientifically substantiated. But this is not such a book; it is a book that is intended to provoke thought and give insight into passion. Therefore, within the context of women and passion, I believe my theory about manic depression is useful, and worth presenting. For the purposes of this chapter, too, I will use the term "manic depression" instead of "bipolar disorder."

WHAT IS MANIC DEPRESSION?

The first order of business is to provide you with a clear understanding of what, exactly, manic depression is. Psychiatrist Peter Breggan, author of *Toxic Psychiatry*, a book that criticizes the current Prozac-pushing model of psychiatry, reminds us that the two states experienced in manic depression—euphoria and melancholy—are completely normal poles of human emotion. Breggan asks us to imagine the emotions of fans watching a baseball game. Within minutes, we see fans shifting from one extreme emotion to the other; one second they're jumping up and down in euphoric joy, and the next second they're wailing in misery. Are all of these fans "sick" because they have a "mood disorder," Breggan asks? He questions the pathologizing of moods to begin with, and eloquently debates whether the cosmetic "mood lift" medicine prescribed to the moody is simply discounting, if not disallowing, normal human emotions to surface. In other words, Breggan asks whether it is right to prescribe drugs that numb our passions.

The image of the passionate baseball fan is not dissimilar to the life of a manic-depressive, who is living in a state of extremes: extreme joy or extreme sorrow. In a sense, it is as though one were living in a state of passion. Studies show that manic depression occurs with greater frequency amongst high-achieving individuals, and may be seen across generations not because of manic genes but because of the special talents and gifts that are inherited across the generations. You see, there is often pressure to achieve in such families. If your father was a brilliant scientist, and your mother was a gifted classical pianist, you may very well feel pressure to succeed in life, or even measure up to your parents' successes.

Episodes of mania are characterized by a speeding up, while the low mood is the biological payback for the bursts of energy, creativity and euphoria seen during the manic period. Manic depression usually surfaces for women during the teenage years or late adolescence—just as women begin to become sexually active and begin to make their way in the world. As a result, it can lead to disastrous consequences in terms of sexual or intimate relationships and career-related decisions. Relationship breakups, job loss, alcohol and drug abuse, and even suicide are common among women who are manic-depressive.

It's important to dispel one of the greatest myths about the highs felt during a period of mania: the myth of productivity. It is generally believed that the highs of manic episodes help one to achieve more, thereby being useful in some way. This just isn't so. The individual who is high may also be busy in very unproductive ways, although she may feel, while she's high, as though she is achieving more and being productive. The truth is, many people in the throes of mania are pretty scattered, unfocused, and can be quite destructive.

Socially, however, the highs may be of tremendous use. A manic woman can be very charismatic, energetic, bubbly and magnetic, making friends easily. For some, manic episodes come complete with all the tools to be a great hostess, party-giver, entertainer or life of the party. Since the senses are heightened in euphoric states, mania also comes in handy if you're a connoisseur of good wine, gourmet food and fresh-cut flowers. For instance, it's not unusual to find manic women to be "dinner party divas"—hosting lavish dinner parties for their friends (in reality, it's a good way for these women to use up their energy cooking, planning, spending, and ultimately, entertaining).

Some women recognize themselves in the signs below, but often it is family members or friends who notice the following signs of manic depression, many of which are associated with indulging the passions:

- erratic behaviour, characterized by wild spending sprees, sexual flings and impulsive acts;

- incredible bursts of energy and activity;

- restlessness (constantly looking for something to do; not able to focus for a long time on one activity);

- fast talking to keep up with a racing mind;

- acting and feeling high or euphoric;

- extreme irritability and distractibility;

- not requiring sleep (you feel there is too much to do in life, and that sleep is a waste of time, even though lack of it may lead to irritability and agitation);

- the belief in unusual or unrealistic abilities and powers (for example, it's not unusual for some women in an episode of mania to believe they are agents of God, or even God Herself);

- making decisions and judgments that seem out of character or "not like her";

- increased need or desire for sex;

- drug abuse (some common culprits: cocaine, alcohol and sleeping pills);

- behaviour that pushes other people's buttons (aggressive or intrusive acts; acting like a "shit disturber");

- total denial that "something's wrong" when confronted;

- increasingly sensitive to sound, and easily irritated by various sounds;

- feeling you are extraordinary or brilliant (even though this may be true!)

- feeling at one with nature, and having heightened senses (everything smells, tastes, sounds, feels and looks beautiful and exquisite);

- being told you are a workaholic because you are taking on too many projects at once;

- calling people all the time for no good reason, and keeping them tied up with useless conversations.

Some experts compare the manic state to being in love—which most of us have experienced at least once. Feminist therapists point out that manic behaviour in women is often the display of "male" traits (arrogance, brashness, wit) that is deemed unacceptable in women. It is indeed ironic that these traits are called "manic" in light of this observations.

Dr. Kay Redfield Jamison, author of the autobiographical *Unquiet Mind*, an account of her own struggles with manic depression, describes her various manic episodes like this:

> At first, everything seemed so easy. I raced about like a crazed weasel, bubbling with plans and enthusiasms, immersed in sports, and staying up all night, night after night, out with friends, reading everything that wasn't nailed down, filling manuscript books with poems and fragments of plays and making expansive, completely unrealistic, plans for my future. The world was filled with pleasure and promise; I felt great. Not just great, I felt *really* great. I felt I could do anything, that no task was too difficult. (Jamison: 36)

And this:

> My normal Brooks Brothers conservatism would go by the board; my hemlines would go up, my neckline down, and I would enjoy the sensuality of my youth. Almost everything was done to excess: instead of buying one Beethoven symphony, I would buy nine; instead of enrolling for five classes, I would enroll in seven; instead of buying two tickets for a concert I would buy eight or ten... (Jamison: 42)

> When I am high I couldn't worry about money if I tried. So I don't. The money will come from somewhere; I am entitled; God will provide. Credit cards are disastrous, personal checks worse. Unfortunately, for manics anyway, mania is a natural extension of the economy. What with credit cards and bank accounts there is little beyond reach. (Jamison: 74)

And this:

> When you're high it's tremendous. The ideas and feelings are fast and frequent like shooting stars, and you follow them until you find better and brighter ones. Shyness goes, the right words and gestures are suddenly there, the power to captivate others a felt certainty. There are interests found in uninteresting people. Sensuality is pervasive and the desire to seduce and be seduced irresistible. Feelings of ease, intensity, power, well-being, financial omnipotence, and euphoria pervade one's marrow. But, somewhere, this

changes. The fast ideas are far too fast, and there are far too many; overwhelming confusion replaces clarity. Memory goes. Humor and absorption on friends' faces are replaced by fear and concern. Everything previously moving with the grain is now against—you are irritable, angry, frightened, uncontrollable, and enmeshed totally in the blackest caves of the mind. (Jamison: 67)

In certain forms of manic depression (bipolar I), the manic episode will typically come on suddenly and quickly, over the course of a few hours or days. And each time a manic episode recurs, it will come on faster and faster. Since these episodes can last anywhere from 4 to 12 months, if untreated, the passions running amok do a lot of damage, destroying personal relationships, jobs or careers, and credit ratings.

Milder forms of mania

The difficulty with understanding manic depression is that we tend to assume that the person suffering from this condition is either "pink" or "blue"—euphoric or depressed; but there are many shades of mood that women with this condition exhibit. For example, the episodes of depression can be mild, moderate or severe, followed by normal moods, followed by a mild mania, known as *hypomania*, which can also turn into extreme mania. People who suffer from hypomania only, rather than the more extreme forms of mania, have what's known as "bipolar II."

There is no single pattern in manic depression, either. Some women may suffer far more from depressive episodes than mania; others may only suffer from occasional depression. And frequently, the depression is combined with mania in a "mixed" state. Milder forms of mania are almost exclusively seen in women.

Women who are hypomanic experience increased energy, a decreased need for sleep and greater than normal self-esteem, although it is not as grandiose as seen in euphoric mania. Irritability and hostility are also common in hypomania.

THE CRASH

The symptoms above will shift as the mood "crashes," and that person will then suffer from a low. As the passion vanishes, the absence of passion, or depression, takes over. The depressive episodes are known as crashes because they generally come on fast, especially when they follow a manic episode. (When people suffer only from depression without mania, depression typically develops slowly and gradually, over the course of several weeks). Here's Kay Redfield Jamison on the subject of her crashes:

> From the time I woke up in the morning until the time I went to bed at night, I was unbearably miserable and seemingly incapable of any kind of joy or enthusiasm. Everything— every thought, word, movement—was an effort. Everything that once was sparkling now was flat. I seemed to myself to be dull, boring, inadequate, thick brained, unlit, unresponsive, chill skinned, bloodless, and sparrow drab. I doubted, completely, my ability to do anything well. It seemed as though my mind had slowed down and burned out to the point of being virtually useless. What is the point in going on like this? I would ask myself. Others would say to me, "It is

only temporary, it will pass, and you will get over it," but of course they had no idea how I felt, although they were certain that they did. Over and over and over I would say to myself, If I can't feel, if I can't move, If I can't think, and I can't care, then what conceivable point is there in living?... Washing my hair took hours to do, and it drained me for hours afterward; filling the ice-cube tray was beyond my capacity, and I occasionally slept in the same clothes I had worn during the day because I was too exhausted to undress... When I was manic, the tempo seemed slow; when I was normal, frenetic seemed fine; when I was depressed, the pace was impossible. (Jamison, *An Unquiet Mind*: 110–11)

Almost Manic: Cyclothymia

Cyclothymia (cyclo-thy-mee-ah) is an even milder form of mania, characterized by the following behaviours which many feminist therapists declare are male behaviours that become pathologized in women:

- *Thrill-seeking behaviour.* This is behaviour that is avoidance-of-life related, demonstrated by promiscuity, substance abuse, gambling or compulsive buying/shopping.

- *Uneven performances in school or work.* In this case, boredom and restlessness have led to a history of numerous career changes, various academic interests and so on. Continually moving to different cities, countless "fresh starts" and "this time things will be different" characterize the lifestyle.

- *Many stormy romantic relationships/marriages.* Your relationships are always in a crisis; you're always struggling with your romantic partner in life, causing a string of failed relationships. You are often the high-maintenance friend in crisis.

- *You have great energy and charm.* Everyone *loves* to be around you—until you become irritable, critical, hostile, easily frustrated and angry over trivial matters. People may describe you as "moody," and you're often "brooding" or depressed.

- *Interfering.* You butt in, uninvited, to your friends' and acquaintances' personal lives. You seem to always know best, even though your own life is a mess. People think you're arrogant or brash.

- *You talk a lot—and go off on tangents.* You have great wit and charm, and are probably a great manipulator when it comes to arguing and defending your point of view. People find it hard to get a word in edgewise, and leave the conversations feeling uneasy, guilty and manipulated.

THE ARTIST AS MADWOMAN

There is a romantic notion that women artists are generally mad, always having breakdowns or committing suicide. There are certainly plenty of emotionally stable artists who do not cross from genius into madness. However, a number of studies show that high levels of creativity and some kinds of mental illness cross paths. There is even thought to be a relationship. Kay Redfield Jamison, in her book *Touched with Fire: Manic Depressive Illness and the Artistic Temperament*, argues that although greater numbers of highly creative people are not found among people with manic-depressive illness, more manic-depressive illness *is* found among highly creative people. This means that if you suffer from manic depression, you don't necessarily have a greater chance of being creative; but if you are highly creative, you have a greater chance of suffering from manic depression. Jamison cites several reputable studies on writers, artists, poets and composers that show a significantly higher rate of manic depression and cyclothymia than in the general population.

Linking manic depression to creativity is not generally accepted. Jamison states that the connection is still a controversial one. The controversy, she maintains, surrounds a misunderstanding of how manic depression affects people's lives. Many of the traits of mania are often attributed to the "artistic temperament," which comprise mood swings or extremes of moods.

Author Gopi Krishna wrote an essay that specifically looked at the relationship between creativity and mood swings, and states that creativity is intertwined with kundilini (lifeforce) energy. Krishna believes that the cycles of elation, which emerge through great productivity, and the cycles of depression, which emerge through periods of nonproductivity, are directly related to the flow of kundalini. (This is the "enlightenment" state we enter, but can also be interpreted as the lifeforce energy the Chinese call the *qi* (pronounced "chi"), or what in the West is known simply as endorphins we make while under stress—what many believe workaholics are addicted to). Krishna writes:

> With the accelerated activity of the evolutionary mechanism, there occurs a tremendous enhancement in the production of life energy or sex energy. When the organism is in perfect condition, the sublimated energy streams into the brain, raising the consciousness to inexpressible heights of oceanic knowledge and rapture. But when the system is impure and the pranic radiation becomes even slightly contaminated, then nature tries to adjust the system in two ways: the radiation either still finds entry into the brain in the contaminated form, leading to anxiety, fear, tension, depression, craving for some kind of excitement or mind-altering drugs or the like. This is the "dark night of the mystic," the depressive, sterile mood of the genius, or a "fit of blues" of the intelligent mind... The other way is by enormously increased pressure at the other end of the evolutionary mechanism—that is, the sexual region—resulting in irrepressible amativeness. (Degler, *The Fiery Muse*: 219–21)

Thomas Moore, author of *Care of the Soul*, reminds us how necessary darker moods are when it comes to the expression of our deep feelings. He believes that melancholy moods can yield great creative work, a time he says, when the soul "embraces its shadow." Human creativity has been defined as a participation in the act of God creating the cosmos. It was once said that "God creates the cosmos, we create the micro-cosmos—the 'human world.'"

One of the best examples of manic depression and creativity in women can be seen in the life of Pulitzer Prize–winning American poet Anne Sexton, who was a contemporary of Sylvia Plath.

She was, at first glance, a typical 1950s suburban housewife. After the birth of her second daughter, Sexton suffered a "suicidal breakdown" (displaying all the symptoms of manic depression). Her therapist suggested she write poetry for therapy purposes. This suggestion led Sexton into literary fame, and many important literary awards over her 18-year career, including the Pulitzer Prize for her third volume of poetry, *Live or Die*—an appropriate title from someone suffering from manic depression.

Sexton's poetry connected many women who felt as disconnected to their housewife role as she did. Sexton, like many women who are manic-depressive, was also an alcoholic. It's been said that her writing, which occurred during her bouts with mania, is what kept her alive; otherwise, she might have ended her life a lot sooner. In the words of Anne Sexton's therapist:

> She felt helpless, unable to function as a wife or mother... Although she was trying her best to live up to the 1950s image of the good wife and mother, she found the task completely beyond her... The sheer existence of the task of writing poetry, through which she could describe her pain, her confusion, and her observations, provided the basis for a critical sense of self-esteem... Once Anne was assured

that she was really able to write poetry, she almost could not stop. Writing poetry became the driving force... (Middlebrook, *Anne Sexton: A Biography*: xiv)

When Sexton would tell her life story for the press, she would compare herself to Snow White: her mother was the queen; the "poisoned apple" was the role she was forced to play in the Boston suburbs; the "poison" was her manic-depressive illness; and the "prince" was her psychiatrist who found the "magic remedy"—poetry. Sexton referred to her poetry as her "rebirth." She was 29, and also, quite possibly, on the verge of her ripening. Evidence of this can be seen in her love poem "The Touch," which is about the resurrection, or rebirth, of her middle-aged body through sex:

> My nerves are turned on. I hear them like
> musical instruments. Where there was silence
> the drums, the strings are incurably playing. You did this.
> Pure genius at work. Darling, the composer has stepped
> into fire.
> (Middlebrook, *Anne Sexton: A Biography*: 3)

Emotional rescue

Through Sexton's story, we can clearly see how her creativity, which was fuelled by her mania, rescued her from the role of housewife. Her "madness" is the only thing, in fact, that kept her sane. Through Anne Sexton's story, we can see the story of many women. Donna who now takes lithium to control her mania, which takes the form, in her words, as "skyrocketing euphoria," shares this:

> My manic episodes surfaced in my late teens (in the early 1980s), as I was struggling with my identity, career choices and so on. My parents were very creative and successful. My father was a film director and my mother was a singer. Nevertheless, I was feeling this pressure to marry one of my boyfriends (I always had several going at once), and have a baby, but the mere thought of that kind of life was worse, I thought, than death itself. *I'd rather be dead than average* was the way I thought.
>
> I don't remember all that went on during my first high, but I recall feeling omniscient. It lasted weeks and weeks. I actually thought that God had chosen me to translate his thoughts to others. I would disappear with my little VW (it was this great '73 white VW) for days, spreading the Gospel of God and telling people I was the Female Christ. It sounds crazy... no, I was completely crazy, but it was so exhilarating, so wonderful. I actually convinced quite a few people of my connection with God, and had a small following for a while. When you're that sure of yourself, even if what you say is insane, people can be swayed by your sheer force of conviction. My parents would always hunt me down though, bring me back, and try to get me to take my lithium. I would do anything to keep my highs, and practically did, including disappearing and living as a stripper for a while.

Milder forms of mania are also salvation from personality expectations, as Laura reveals:

> When I wasn't manic, I felt very passive and felt as though no one cared what I had to say. But when I was manic, this incredible life and bubble would come through my eyes. People could tell when I was manic and started to call my moods my "on" and "off" personalities. My highs were virtually an escape from myself. I wasn't crazed the way some manics are, but I was definitely much more interesting manic than not. My mania also showed me that men are attracted to something inner rather than outer. When I was high, I could attract anyone I wanted; there was no one I couldn't meet. And it didn't matter to the men, when I was manic, whether I was a size 6 or a size 10. [*Note*: Laura's weight often fluctuated between mood swings.]

The "mania to the rescue" theme can also be seen in the life of writer Sylvia Plath, who is best known for her somewhat autobiographical novel *The Bell Jar*. Plath committed suicide in 1963 at age 30. She had also been a victim of old-style psychiatry in the form of electroshock therapy, which she was receiving during the 1950s. In one of her last poems she writes: "The blood jet is poetry,/There is no stopping it." (Stevenson, *Bitter Fame*: xi)

Plath, like Sexton, also struggled with her role expectations. In her late teens and early 20s, Plath rejected the sorority girl role, which she was able to play when she needed to, but secretly loathed. She describes her peers in this prose:

"What did these picked buds of American womanhood do at their sorority meetings? They ate cake; ate cake and catted about the Saturday night date."

Plath also struggled in her mid to late 20s with the housewife role, which was apparently aggravated by her husband, Ted Hughes, also a writer, who some believe was very destructive for Plath (it is rumoured, for example, that he appropriated much of Plath's work). Plath always felt that her role as mother and housewife took her away from her writing. Like Sexton, Plath needed to be able to write in order to express her emotions. It is believed that when she was robbed of the opportunity to write because of her responsibilities to her children, she suffered terribly.

Typical writing when Plath was high included:

> I am full of poems; my joy whirls in tongues of words... I know myself, in vigor and prime and growing, and know I am strong enough to keep myself whole, no matter what... I have never been so exultant... What a huge humor we have, what running strength! (Stevenson, *Bitter Fame*: 87)

But, with her mania, came intense sexual desires, too. She was considered highly sexual by her time's standards, given to seeing two or three men at once (usually in different cities). She would refer to her sexual sojourns away as her "wicked" weekends. One of her most famous poems, "Pursuit," was about the "dark forces of lust," which was a bit of a shocker for 1956. It's been said of "Pursuit" that Plath's own fury was expressed through her sexual desires. Another poem illus-trates her intensity with protecting her sexual prey:

> The vampire is there, too. The old, primal hate. That desire to go round castrating the arrogant ones who become such chil-dren in the moment of passion… I fight all women for my men. My men. I am a woman, and there is no loyalty, even between mother and daughter. Both fight for the father, for the son, for the bed of mind and body. (Stevenson, *Bitter Fame:* 71)

The absence of a creative outlet is, for the creative woman, a passionless, meaningless existence. Virginia Woolf, most famous for her novel *A Room of One's Own*, considered a liter-ary genius, filled her pockets with rocks and drowned herself. She, too, suffered from manic depression.

SOCIAL TRIGGERS FOR MANIA

When I was about 12, I remember being fascinated with *Sybil,* a book about one of the first cases of extreme multiple personality disorders. Today, psychiatrists and other mental health experts agree that childhood abuse triggers this condi-tion. In other words, there is a social trigger for MPD—not a brain chemistry disorder. Life circumstances become so over-whelming or horrific, the child's mind (the condition usually manifests in childhood) actually creates another "self"—or as many as it needs—to take over, while the waking self—the original self—escapes. A part of me was envious of this talent, and felt dismay that I was forced to endure my childhood alone—without the help of other selves to take over.

In exploring manic-depressive illness in women, I suggest that similar social triggers are at work: the manic state is one that rescues women from the passionless lives they are forced to unwillingly lead due to unfair social arrangements; by this, I mean societal roles that can be stifling emotionally and intellectually, particularly for creative women.

Mania can also rescue women from their bodies, enabling them to feel powerful and beautiful in spite of impossible beauty standards. Moreover, it can rescue them from impossible expectations. These expectations are known as the backlash of feminism (once known as women's liberation). What have so-called liberated women gained? Many feminists argue that all that's happened is that women have entered the male world on male terms which, for many women, involves deep sacrifices. The notion of the liberated career woman who has it all has simply led to a new impossible "fulfillment norm"—the SuperWoman phenomenon (sometimes known as SuperMom).

The SuperWoman is beautiful, thin, successful, with the perfect husband and family. She chose just the right career, and chose to have children at just the right time—biologically. She has no problem fulfilling her dual roles as lawyer, doctor or accountant by day, perfect homemaker by night. The SuperWoman of today is perhaps as dangerous an ideal as the Perfect Homemaker of the mid–twentieth century. SuperWoman sends the message that women can have it all in a world where we not only *cannot* have it all, but often have not much, if anything.

And with SuperWoman comes the supermodel—a 17-year-old girl whose image is distorted by computers, lighting and deceptive photography, who is supposed to be what a 35-year-old woman should strive to look like. The worst legacy of supermodels is that a woman still makes more money with her body than her mind, and little girls grow up preferring to look like skeleton-thin Kate Moss and become models than strive towards meaningful careers. Since the corporate world is still a masculine world, a masculine body type has become the feminine ideal.

How far have women come in the workplace, anyway? Here are the latest statistics, from the U.S. Census Bureau (U.S. Dept. of Commerce), Status of Women Canada, Statistics Canada, the Feminist Majority Foundation, and the Centre for the Study of Women in Society: the average female worker in the U.S. earns 76 (71 Cdn.) cents for every dollar a man earns. Only 2.6 percent of corporate officers in Fortune 500 companies are women; 4.3 percent of corporate officers are women in the Fortune Service 500 in spite of the fact that 61 percent of all service workers are women. It's estimated that at the current rate of increase, it will take until the year 2466 before women reach equality with men in the executive suite.

In Canada, the average female worker earns 63.8 percent for every dollar a man earns, and Canadian women still do the largest share of unpaid work, which was last estimated at 65 percent in 1992. Examples of unpaid work include meal preparation, cleaning, child care and volunteer work. And even though women make up 40 percent of the workforce, 16 percent of working men are self-employed, compared to 8 percent of working women. Female entrepreneurs still have more difficulty securing business loans and financing from banking institutions than male entrepreneurs.

It's also worth noting that there is still inadequate daycare for millions of North American families, which often forces women out of the workplace.

Kay Redfield Jamison writes:

> This pattern of shifting moods and energies had a very seductive side to it, in large part because of fitful reinfusions of the intoxicating moods that I enjoyed in high school. These were quite extraordinary, filling my brain with a cataract of ideas and more than enough energy to give me at least the illusion of carrying them out... (Jamison, *An Unquiet Mind*: 42)

The unwillingness to give up the highs felt in manic depression is a classic struggle, as Jamison reveals:

> Long after my psychosis cleared, and the medications took hold, it became part of what one remembers forever, surrounded by an almost Proustian melancholy. Long since that extended voyage of my mind and soul, Saturn and its icy rings took on an elegiac beauty, and I don't see Saturn's image now without an acute feeling of sadness at its being so far away from me, so unobtainable in so many ways. The intensity. Glory, and absolute assuredness of my mind's flight made it very difficult for me to believe, once I was better, that the illness was one I should willingly give up... but if you have had stars at your feet and the rings of planets through your hands, are used to sleeping only four or five hours a night and now sleep eight, are used to staying up all night for days and weeks in a row and now cannot,

it is a very real adjustment to blend into a three-piece-suit schedule, which, while comfortable to many, is new, restrictive, seemingly less productive, and maddeningly less intoxicating. (Jamison, *An Unquiet Mind*: 9,92)

Jamison was herself an artist, and also more appreciative of the arts when she was manic. She would write poetry, listen to music differently and see paintings with much more clarity and depth. Mania, it can be argued, is a creative, artistic state. It is a state that enables a woman to live passionately— however brief—instead of fading into the suburban or "female role" wasteland that threatens her soul.

In chapter 3, we see the social triggers for depression, which is a flatness that pervades after years in passionless relationships, marriages, jobs and routine. In this chapter, we see the same social triggers for mania which, for a smaller group of women (usually very creative women), was a clever escape route from the experience of being female in a restrictive social structure.

Although I, myself, have never experienced mania, I must admit I am attracted to others who do experience it. I, too, wish I could live in an exalted state, where I had confidence and self-worth. What a wonderful feeling that would be.

For a more clinical look at the types of manic depression, or bipolar disorder, and treatment available, see my book Women and Sadness: A Sane Approach To Depression.

5

UNHEALTHY PASSIONS

VIOLENCE, OBSESSIONS, SECRETS AND LIES

Many of us will go to crazy places to find passion (defined in chapter 1 as "feeling your life")—places that ultimately have bad consequences. Many women will wander into abusive relationships. Many women in unsatisfying relationships will wander into affairs of the bed (meaning, a full-fledged sexual relationship), affairs of the heart (meaning, an unrequited yearning for a relationship with someone who is unavailable) or affairs of the mind (meaning, becoming obsessed with an object of desire regardless of whether the relationship is requited).

Cybersex and pornography can both play a role in these situations, but for women, cybersex is not used in the same way as it is for men; women will wander into e-mail relationships (frequently by way of dating sites or chat rooms), while men tend to use "quick fix" pornography sites, currently rated as the most frequently visited sites on the Internet (health sites come second). Women may also be vulnerable to becoming objects of male obsessions and fantasy in exchange for the attention and flattery, which is also a pretty crazy place to be in.

Because we wander into these situations unconsciously, these relationships can become so dangerous and unfulfilling, our lives or reputations can even be at risk. At best, unhealthy passions lead us down a dramatic and unsatisfying spiral that is fodder for trash talk shows. This chapter will first explore why we go to crazy places by looking more closely at women's misguided anger. It will then explore the complex webs we can weave when we're looking for passion. Understanding why we go to these places is the first place to start if you want to leave the place you're in.

WOMEN, PASSION AND UNEXPRESSED ANGER

Anger is one of the most vital expressions of passion. However, women are not allowed to openly express their anger unless it's in the interest of someone, or something else: a child, a partner or a cause. Many women turn anger inward, and it manifests as depression. When this doesn't happen, the anger becomes misdirected and confused, spawning all kinds of negative behaviours and relationships.

Films traditionally heralded as "women and anger" films include *Thelma and Louise* and, of course, *Fatal Attraction*. One of the best examples of a woman's anger in film can be seen in *Presumed Innocent*. In this film, Harrison Ford is accused of murdering a colleague with whom he had a passionate affair. His wife (played by Bonnie Bedelia) remains in the background as the devoted spouse who silently suffered through his affair but chose to stay with him. We learn, too, that she left a promising academic career as a mathematics professor (she is still working on her Ph.D.). She graduated at the top of her class, but notes that while the math whiz second in the class just made full professor, she is still making beds.

We think the film will end, leaving us unsure about who the real killer is, but when Ford finds the murder weapon in his shed, yet remains completely puzzled, the plot twists one last time into what is supposed to be unbelievable but, in fact, is more believable than the filmmaker probably intended: yep, the wife is the killer. But all women secretly applaud her actions because of her explanation.

When Bedelia becomes a "non person" as a result of the affair between Ford and Satchi, she gets more and more resentful and angry. She says she began to plan her own suicide (traditionally turning the anger inward) until the dream appeared. In this dream, it is the destroyer—Satchi—who is destroyed. "Now that's a dream worth living for," the wife notes. She plans Satchi's murder quietly, and carries it out, describing the feelings of power she has when she is engaged in the act of killing. She is murdering in self-defence: she wants her life back. The murder victim is actually the character we feel the least sympathy for. She was a manipulative woman who "got what she deserved."

The implicit message of the film is that when women are aggressive, and go after what they want, they are unacceptable. The unacceptable woman—the woman whose sin is behaving too "male" (she sleeps around; she's manipulative and self-serving)—is killed; the acceptable woman, the passive, submissive woman who gives up her life for a man, is redeemed. The broader theme of the film, however, is about the danger of women's unexpressed anger; in this case it explodes into rage and violence. However, the fact is, for most women, anger is rarely expressed in normal or acceptable ways. It usually comes out inappropriately: masked and twisted.

Common manifestations of women's anger include:

- *Depression.* Depression in women is commonly under-stood as "anger turned inward." Anger is mobilizing; depression is immobilizing.

- *Eating disorders.* Women will often use food to suppress, or, alternatively, express, their anger.

- *Self-harm.* This is a broad category that includes harmful addictions, harmful relationships, suicide attempts, self-mutilation, self-destructive or self-sabotaging behaviours.

- *Harming others.* This is a broad category that includes petty crimes, such as theft; "vexatious lies" (lies that deliberately hurt versus white lies); harassment (stalking, repeated phone calls or e-mails); violence against children (women's powerlessness can be turned against those with even less power—their children); heinous crimes (murder, or extreme violence against others).

How we choose to display our anger has a lot to do with what we witnessed as children in our mothers' behaviours. For example, Angela has been dealing with substance abuse since her early teens, and wanders into relationships with violent men. A lot of her behaviour, one could say, was learned, evidenced through this memory she shares:

> In my house, anger was allowed for the men but not for the women. My father yelled; my mother drank. The more my father yelled at my mother, the more she drank. She also smoked very heavily, and had a habit of drinking herself into a stupor with a cigarette in hand. On more than one occasion, I would find her asleep with a burning cigarette. I used to think: "She's so mad at the world, she's just going to burn the house down." One day, I sneaked into her bedroom and stole her cigarettes. I opened them up one by one and shredded all of the tobacco into the toilet. When she caught me doing it, she yanked me so hard, my shoulder was dislocated. I was so ashamed I told everyone I fell.

Christine has a history of wandering into relationships with unavailable men, which robs her of self-worth. She has spent many nights planning her suicide, and in her adult years, began drinking. She recalls the following:

> It was not until I was in my late teens that I realized my father was cheating on my mother. I just recall that he was always away; rarely home for supper... just not around. One of my earliest memories is being woken up by terrible shouting, and finding my mother and father rolling on the floor with a knife. At first it looked like my mother was trying to kill him, but then it became clear that he was trying to prevent her from stabbing herself. She kept saying, "Leave

me alone; let me die, let me die." My father committed her to a psychiatric ward shortly after that incident and told my sister and I that she was crazy, and that if we saw her again, she would kill us.

Jo-Ann has a history of passive-aggressive relationships with both men and women. What is meant by "passive-aggressive" here is that she will deliberately end all of her relationships by setting up inappropriate conflicts that she refuses to resolve. A missed appointment, for example, might be met with an e-mail accusing the appointment misser of "betraying her" or "ruining her life." She uses e-mail and voice mail to lash out at those who have disappointed her (and it doesn't take much!). But then, she will not return calls (she screens them) or e-mails when the person on the receiving end of her e-mails or voice mails tries to resolve the conflict, which often leads them to becoming enraged. As a result, Jo-Ann has attracted a string of unhealthy obsessive males into her life, who try to get even with her. She's been the victim of obscene calls, the recipient of dead animals and dead flowers, and oddly, the object of desire for men who secretly thrive on the conflict. Jo-Ann admitted to me that she learned to dodge conflict in childhood: "When my father wanted to hurt me, he wouldn't beat me; he would beat my dog."

Self-mutilation

There is now a growing awareness about a dark secret some women bear, which speaks volumes about unexpressed anger. Some women physically harm themselves by deliberately cutting themselves, burning themselves, scraping, banging and bruising themselves. This is known technically as self-mutilation. Therapists who work with women who self-mutilate say it is not surprising for such a woman to show up at the session bleeding or even dripping with blood. Often alcohol and drugs play a role in the self-mutilation, as they numb the pain, enabling more serious wounds.

Wounds can be so severe that women may cut themselves right to the bone, inflict second-degree burns on one or many parts of their bodies. Many women also cut around their genitals. Women who do this are often survivors of sexual abuse, where they inappropriately take control over the battery or abuse.

Experts in the study of self-mutilation believe that through abuse and trauma, the woman has become so numb to her feelings, her mutilation acts prove to her that she is feeling, human, or "feeling her life." The self-wounding validates her humanity, her ability to feel her flesh. On the flip side, she may be feeling so much from her trauma, the wounds are a distraction. By feeling physical pain from her wounds, she can be distracted from her emotional pain. There is also the element of voice through the wounds. When women cannot speak about their abuse, the wounds speak *for* them. Rose, a therapist, shares this:

> A lot of women who cut themselves sort of split off during the mutilating act; they "discover themselves" cutting, or don't even remember the cutting and just "discover themselves" bleeding. How much they're really awake or aware of the

act is unknown, because many, out of shame, will deny that they are knowingly doing this to themselves. It's a very tricky problem in terms of how to work with these women. But when a therapist tries to stop her from harming herself by bringing in social services, calling 911, or whatever, it often fuels the acts of mutilation and makes it worse. I prefer to *listen* to the wounds, which is the voice of the woman. She also has a right to cut her body if she wants, and I respect that she is trying to tell me something with her actions.

Why we can't get angry

Because many women play a subordinate role in society, they can develop a belief system that makes it difficult for them to express anger. Many women believe the following:

1.   I am weak. If I express my anger, I'll be overpowered.

2.   I am dependent. If I express my anger, I may disrupt my lifestyle.

3.   I have no right to feel anger. If I express my anger, I won't be liked or loved as much. (This belief is an extension of feelings of low self-worth and self-esteem.)

4.   I want people to think I'm nice. I don't want to be labelled a bitch or a nag or bitter. (This belief stems from negative stereotypes associated with angry women.)

Women also suffer when they feel they are disconnected to the world around them. Therefore, anger may threaten to sever their relationships, and so they may go to great lengths to mask their anger. Many women rank having a relationship more valuable than having a self. As a result, terms such as "de-selfing" and "silencing of the self" are used in academic articles and books focusing on women and anger.

De-selfing or silencing of the self means that your whole value system (what you think and want) is "up for sale" in order to keep the peace in your relationships. The flip side is that when we do this long enough, we become very angry. De-selfing or silencing of the self is considered to be at the root of most women's inability to express anger. In the most horrifying example, the infamous women from the Manson family (the female followers of crazed murderer Charles Manson), responsible for the Sharon Tate murders in 1969, were willing to kill for him rather than upset their relationships with him and uphold their own value system.

A more commonplace example of de-selfing is in this tale from Julie:

> When I first got involved with Bruce, he was up front about his drug dealing, which he softened by saying that he was just a nice guy "helping out some friends." Even though I felt his dealing was wrong, I never said anything. I didn't want to make him angry, and I was willing to put up with it in order to keep him. One day, he took me with him on a deal (he was selling ecstasy or "E"). As he drove to the buyer's house, I remember getting very angry to the point of just

seething. I stopped talking, and told him that I would wait in the car. He kept asking me if I was mad; he kept trying to find out why I wouldn't talk. I just kept saying, "Nothing; it's nothing."

A few months later, he asked me if I would lie for him and say he was with me when he wasn't. I asked him for details, but he wouldn't disclose them. When I said I wouldn't help him, he accused me of being unfaithful, and betraying him. The next morning, I called a taxi, and had the driver help me move all of my things out of Bruce's place. I went to a girlfriend's. I just left Bruce without saying goodbye... without an explanation. It was easier. But then I felt really guilty, and worried that he wouldn't love me anymore.

Even when we are justified to feel anger, we feel guilt. Harriet Lerner, author of *The Dance of Anger*, writes:

'See no evil, hear no evil, speak no evil' becomes the unconscious rule for those of us who must deny the awareness and expression of our anger. The 'evil' that we must avoid includes any number of thoughts, feelings, and actions that might bring us into open conflict, or even disagreement, with important others. To obey this rule, we must become sleepwalkers. We must not see clearly, think precisely, or remember freely. The amount of creative, intellectual, and sexual energy that is trapped by this need to express anger and remain unaware of its sources is simply incalculable. (Lerner: 7,8)

It is frequently de-selfing that is behind a woman staying in an abusive or violent situation. Here is a story Melanie shares about emotional abuse and de-selfing:

> When I married Ben, we were both reformed Jews; we went to synagogue during the High Holidays; we celebrated the Jewish holidays with our families, and other than that, life was pretty normal and suburban. After 11 years of marriage, Ben was going through what I think was a midlife crisis; he was feeling unfulfilled, and we actually had discussed separating at one time. But because we had three children, we decided to stay together.
>
> He started to get involved with an ultra-orthodox Jewish sect that I felt was fanatical. Within a few months, Ben wanted the family to transform into an orthodox Jewish family, which involved tremendous effort and sacrifice for me. I could no longer wear normal clothes, and had to always wear a skirt of a certain length as well as a wig; he wanted our children to leave their public school and go to an ortho-dox school; he wouldn't allow my family members over anymore because they weren't kosher and wouldn't allow us to go to my family members' homes for the same reasons. Ben completely isolated me from my support system.
>
> Then he wouldn't allow me to cook without supervision from other orthodox women, and even installed a second kitchen (one kitchen was to be used for cooking dairy, the other for cooking meat). I fought him on every change, but each battle was harder. He got more fanatical and accused

me of going against God and the word of God; he would rant and rave. I gave in. I lived as though I was acting in a bad play.

My sisters and brothers were very upset and tried to get me to leave him, but I wouldn't. We no longer practised birth control, and I got pregnant again. One day, as my protest, I served a pork roast to Ben, who at first didn't recognize what he was eating. When I told him it was pork, he got up, picked me up, and literally removed me from my house and the children without saying a word. Just before he slammed the door, he ripped his clothing and said the Jewish prayer for the dead. I screamed outside the house for hours, crying and begging to come back in, apologizing… degrading myself. A neighbour came out and took me into her house. She called my sister for me, and I lived there for three months.

I am now divorced and Ben keeps me from my children, with the support of the orthodox Jewish community behind him, claiming that I am a bad influence on them.

FATAL ATTRACTIONS AND DOMESTIC VIOLENCE

Many women have openly said that they are attracted to angry men because they can't express their own anger. In the context of women and passion, it is quite possible that women who are looking for feelings and depth of emotion in their relationships may pass on the Trade and make a deal with the devil instead.

The "devil"—the abuser—studies show, displays a very predictable pattern of behaviour: he swings from long periods of Mr. Wonderful—where he is attentive, romantic and very sexually satisfying, to periods, sometimes brief, sometimes long, of Mr. Terrible—where he is violent, angry, abusive, controlling, displaying terrible jealousy and rage. Each reappearance of Mr. Wonderful becomes intensified, as the make-up sex becomes more intense. A good man, for many women, is not as hard to find as good sex, which is what keeps a lot of women in abusive relationships. Many experts on the subject of violence and sex insist that hostility generates and enhances sexual excitement. To some, sex might even be considered a form of warfare, with the theme of divide and conquer played out in the bedroom.

It is my belief that women make an unconscious "deal to feel." The logic in choosing such a partner, of course, is flawed, and the relationship very destructive, but given the limited number of "curtains" available for women, it's not that illogical a choice. Some women may look at Curtain #1—The Trade, and opt, instead, for Curtain #2—The Deal with the Devil. At least, with Curtain #2, they get some good sex, and are exposed to feeling rather than to a passionless existence.

Study after study on domestic violence show that women in violent relationships come from all kinds of backgrounds: from nurturing to abusive. Women in these relationships can be highly educated, in professions such as doctors, lawyers, professors; they can also be poorly educated, according to most stereotypes. Ironically, it is the women with less education and money who have more social support systems in place to leave. Women with higher education and more money tend to stay in abusive relationships much longer because they are afraid to admit what's going on in their house. They stay out of shame, as Karen reveals:

To outsiders, our marriage looked ideal, and at first it was idyllic. I thought Luke was the most wonderful man I could hope for, and our physical relationship was incredible. Things started to turn when we went into our fifth year of marriage. Luke insisted that I give up my own bank account and deposit my paycheque into his, so we could live as a "family" not as "roommates."

He then started to question my requests for money—especially when it was for personal needs, such as clothing or getting my hair done. I walked around looking like I was living on welfare half the time. Then Luke would turn around, give me a credit card and carte blanche on what I could spend, but when I came home with new things, he would question my taste, and tell me certain things were ugly or "not sexy at all."

He would fly into rages over small things. He never beat me up, but he would grab me, shove me, and most frequently break things around the house that I cared about, like my grandmother's china. This behaviour would go on for a few weeks and then the old Luke would return. He would take me out and we would celebrate the "return." I once suggested that he might be manic-depressive, and thought

> he should get some help, but that only triggered another
> rage: "If I'm manic-depressive, it's because of *you*... *you*
> made me like this."
>
> I began to feel so much shame and embarrassment over my
> marriage and what it had become that I stopped seeing my
> friends. I just withdrew and told them family-illness lies. I
> said my mother was having surgery; my father was ill; I had
> chronic fatigue, bronchitis, and things like that.

The typical pattern in domestic abuse is for the abuser to begin to establish control over the woman through verbal putdowns. By the time battering begins, the woman feels so degraded and helpless, she doesn't have the emotional strength to leave. As mentioned above, even women with fame, money and success can find themselves in these relationships. One of the most chilling examples is the life of Ali MacGraw.

In 1970, Ali MacGraw was a superstar with a storybook life. She was the Julia Roberts of her day, having just made all women cry and melt in *Love Story*. MacGraw was beautiful, smart (and not afraid to express it), talented, and married to one of Hollywood's most powerful executives, Robert Evans.

In her next film after *Love Story*, she began a passionate romance with the legendary actor Steve McQueen. To outsiders, she was living a dream. But her nightmare had only just begun. Incredibly, MacGraw gave up her acting career (at its peak no less) to please the volatile, demanding, alcoholic McQueen. It was a classic case of an abusive male partner establishing control. McQueen essentially made MacGraw his prisoner. He influenced MacGraw to drink, which is an extremely common pattern among abusers. MacGraw was passed over by McQueen at 40 for a younger 20-something woman who bore a startling resemblance to MacGraw.

MacGraw left McQueen without money or a career, and then began a dangerous pattern of sex addiction. MacGraw's own words shed light on the mindset of a woman trapped in abuse:

> For a long time I convinced myself that I was a very free spirit when it came to my relationships with men. I concocted some kind of warped feminist jargon to tell myself that I was not only open and available, but also admirably straightforward. The truth is, for decades I was incapable of any real intimacy except for sex. Most of the rest of my behavior was pretty controlled, including my so-called honesty. (MacGraw: 145)

There are hundreds of Hollywood stories like MacGraw's. In fact, women who are successful are often most vulnerable to abuse by their partners, who at first are attracted by the talent and success, but then want to control or crush it. In the well-publicized relationship of Ike and Tina Turner, Tina left a long-term abusive relationship with Ike Turner, walking away with mere pocket change.

Men and anger

Men display their anger in very different ways than women. In fact, they are encouraged to display aggression, and boys are even made to fear the consequences of not being aggressive. Throughout history, regardless of their own positions in the world, men have always been able to own women and children, and because of their size and strength, men have always been able to intimidate women with the threat of violence.

New research from Shere Hite on sex and violence reveals that many men begin to associate violence with sex at puberty, when societal pressures make them reject their mothers—a woman they love more than any other. When a 12- or 13-year-old boy tells his mother to shut up in front of his friends, he is asserting dominance to avoid being called a sissy or a mama's boy. The rejection of the mother is painful for the boy, but a necessary rite of passage to assert his dominance in his culture. This is what some researchers believe is behind the puzzling male behaviour of being passionate, loving and desirous one day, and cold, hostile, aggressive and violent the next. In essence, men tend to combine their need for sex with the need to keep women distant.

Confusion also results over the mother's reaction to this rejection. Many mothers become more understanding when their sons reject them, which apparently sends the message to some young men that women love pain. But many men, in fact, feel tremendous guilt over deserting their mothers, and in their sexual relationships with women can become enraged when they hear their "mother" calling through the needs or wants of their partners.

Sam Keen, author of *The Passionate Life*, refers to "erotic poverty," which can also contribute to violent behaviour. According to Keen, when men are deprived of bonding experiences in childhood, it contributes to violent behaviour.

Inappropriate sexuality can develop in men when appropriate affection is not shown to them early enough.

Men are also encouraged to compete, to be better, or the best at something. Thus, when they are angry, their need to feel "better" by *being* better fuels their verbal abuse, as Carla's story illustrates:

> Mark would always downgrade my work as a graphic designer by telling me that my working at home was not as productive, or as important, as his going to an office each day. And because my work was freelance, and his work earned a regular paycheque, he would constantly refer to his money as more valued, and more integral to a household where I, in fact, contributed just as much.

> His anger would rage at night and in the morning; he would complain that I kept him up with my wheezing (I have asthma), and because of that, he'd probably lose his job because of poor performance. He would always say: *You can just sleep in, but I have to go to work like a normal, responsible person."* I would try to argue that my job was just as valid, even though I worked from home, and pointed out how many times I got up at 5:00 a.m. to finish a project, or worked until 2:00 a.m. My objections fell on deaf ears.

> Because he hated his job so much, he would get much more irritable at night. One night, I was tossing and turning, and began wheezing. I reached for my asthma puffer, and Mark sat bolt upright in bed, his face red with rage. He put his hands around my neck and said: "I can't sleep because of

YOU. SHUT UP... SHUT UP... SHUT UP... YOU FUCKING
BITCH... YOU'RE RUINING MY LIFE... IF IT WASN'T FOR
YOU AND THIS FUCKING MORTGAGE, I COULD QUIT
MY JOB!" I was frequently kicked out of our bedroom and
made to sleep on the couch because my sleep wasn't as
important as his.

Gloria Steinem maintains that the more incomplete a
woman feels (because of low self-esteem), the more needy she
becomes for male approval. She projects all of her missing
qualities onto the man. Abuse is perpetuated by the woman's
need for this approval, and the man's need to prove he's *better*.
The projections can lead into other negative circumstances
such as obsessions.

OBSESSIONS AND LOVE ADDICTION

Obsessions, in the context of women and passion, refer to
being continuously preoccupied with another person.
Obsessions usually arise when a romantic interest goes unrequited. Usually, you are investing the object of your obsession
with more than s/he deserves, and the obsessions are built
around fantasy and your own need for fulfillment. The obsession is really a distraction from looking at more important
issues in your life, or root causes of your unfulfillment.

Women who become obsessed are usually in the throes of
an unhappy, dispassionate life, and they obsess as a way to
escape; it is, in a sense, a passionate escape, except instead of

feeling your life you start to feel someone else's life more profoundly than your own. You're so caught up, in fact, with someone else's life that you forget about living your own. Most women silently obsess, as Simone shares:

Tony and I were just friends, but I longed for more, and wondered if he felt the same way about me as I did about him. I would spend hours analyzing his e-mails, looking for hints of romantic subtext. If he signed off with a "take care" one day instead of a "cheers," I would think for hours and hours about why he carefully chose to deviate from one sign-off over another. Why was he inserting a happy face at a certain point in the e-mail versus another point?

I would save his voice messages and play them back, over and over, looking for "clues" of his interest in me. I would then spend hours crafting e-mails to him, taking my time to carefully word things so he wouldn't guess how I felt. When I would send an e-mail, I would check every 10 minutes for a response, and be devastated if I didn't get one right away, or elated when it arrived.

This is how I spent my time for months. I would apparently talk about Tony all the time to my friends; I would take every opportunity to insert his name into conversations when I could. If he tentatively suggested we go for a beer or something, I would carefully plan my wardrobe for hours—days before we would meet. I never realized how destructive it all was until one day I lost the ability to work.

When obsessions are requited, they become romantic rescues. But because the romance is based in unreality instead of reality, it cannot be sustained, and can lead to serial obsessions and romance, which experts call love addiction. The term "addiction" refers to an activity or substance that bolsters you in some way, or gives you a high.

Being high on romance is what drives people into wandering from one relationship into another. The romantic is looking for an impossible ideal: her fantasy, which is usually hard to find. She manufactures fiction around a person, and idealizes that individual.

Women have different fantasies than men about romance; women want to be involved and connected, and are looking for long-term satisfaction. Men, on the other hand, are looking for short-term relationships with big returns.

Sam Keen says of pornography: "The appeal of pornography (or serial sex/love addicted relationships) is the magical promise (always broken) of passion without involvement—you can be shaken to ecstasy without touching another embodied human being." This is why love addicts usually can't find satisfaction: each partner wants something else: the woman wants connection; the man wants the fruits of connection without the labour.

Ali MacGraw shares her experiences with romance addiction:

> I was totally out of touch with who I was, yet I fooled myself into thinking I was refreshingly uninhibited. Lots of times, I was, if not flat-out drunk, at least thoroughly buzzed, because, I guess, I was a lot more frightened than I real-

ized. And if I was not high on alcohol, I was certainly high on my favorite concoction, Romance... Romance, for me, was usually just heat. There was one relationship I entered into because I knew I wanted to be taken care of, and there were others I fell into because I guess that on some subconscious level I wanted to explore different facets of my own personality. More than once, I know I got into a relationship to test just how crazy I could get... I am stunned to realize that my compulsion is sometimes controllable in the alcohol department, but not in the sexual arena. I am desperate to be held, to be convinced that I am worth loving. And while I honestly believe that I love in return with more than my share, I am starting to question my motives. (MacGraw, *Moving Pictures*: 145, 161)

In craving rescue and connection, women may wander into relationships with love/sex addicts unwittingly, as Su Lin did:

I met Sam during a business travel flight. I had just been through a horrendous year stresswise, and actually had not been with a man for a long time. Sam was quite charming, and a little bit of a taboo for me because he was African-American; all of the men of colour I knew were from the Caribbean. He told me that I was "exotic" to him because I was Chinese.

At first the relationship started like any other: we both made it clear that we were attracted to each other, and exchanged business cards, home numbers and e-mails after the flight. When I got home, an e-mail was already waiting for me, which was a bit suggestive, but in the realm of playful. The next e-mail was graphic, and I literally sucked in my breath in shock when I read it. A part of me was flattered; it was nice to be wanted and desired. Sam called me shortly after the e-mail, and the conversation was normal: a "getting to know you" sort of call. We talked about feelings, backgrounds and so on. I was really starting to like him.

Then the next call was strange. He called and asked me how I like to "touch myself" and seemed to be engaging me in a game of phone sex. I wasn't comfortable, but somehow felt that perhaps I was just being a prude. I played along, all the while really revolted with myself. He abruptly hung up (when he was about to climax), just like men do when they dial 976 lines.

The pattern of intermittent normal calls spliced in between these sexual calls persisted, and I kept avoiding the sexual calls, telling him it wasn't a great time for me. I also caught him in some lies, and decided he was untrustworthy. When I stopped returning his calls, Sam started to call me at odd hours—when I was asleep, 6:00 a.m., 1:00 a.m., and so on. He would tell me that he thought of me all the time; thought I could "touch his soul" and that he longed for my "China doll pussy." Warning bells were going off in my head, but somehow, I kept thinking there was some value in him.

A few months later, when we were in the same city, we met in his hotel room (I had actually avoided meeting him for months because I was so ambivalent about my feelings). I was sure I would at least be treated to a romantic adventure. Instead, he just flung me on the bed, entered me a few times and came, without even asking me how the experience was for me. The experience was painfully empty, and it took me a while to sort out whose emptiness I was feeling: mine, his or the experience itself. But before I had time to really think, he got up, put on his pants and said: "I thought we were going to have this great spiritual connection, but it's not happening. You're nice, but not right for my soul. I'd like you to leave." I was baffled at the lengths Sam had gone to seduce me (all the phone calls, e-mails, cards), compared to the amount of time it took him to dismiss me. (Our sojourn lasted exactly two hours; a one-hour drinks/bar session, followed by a one-hour sex session in his hotel room).

I left his hotel room angry with myself, and confused, but sent him an abrupt note telling him that spiritual connections take two, and that I, for one, was not about to connect with a man who did not earn my trust. He replied by e-mail and said that I was "bitter" and that he was sorry I felt that way—completely ignoring that I had a right to be angry. I felt as if I had been treated like garbage; but the truth is, all that happened is that I allowed a piece of garbage to enter me in a moment of weakness for the "romance." I wanted to be romanced, and I got fucked instead.

A few years later, a much older female friend (who had been around) told me that any man who likes to talk dirty in his letters or phone calls is a man with a lot of problems, and one that should be avoided at all costs.

Even the founder of *Ms. Magazine*, Gloria Steinem, is not immune to romance addiction. She explains:

> So I reverted to a primordial skill that I hadn't used since feminism had helped me to make my own life: getting a man to fall in love with me. As many women can testify, this is alarmingly easy, providing you're willing to play down who you are and play up who he wants you to be. In this case, I was aided by my travel and his work and social schedule, which left us with little time to find out how very different we were. And also by something I didn't want to admit: a burnout and an erosion of self so deep that outcroppings of a scared sixteen-year-old had begun to show through. Like a friend who lost weight and, with the burning away of her body fat, re-experienced an anesthetic that had been stored in it from an operation years before, I had lost so much energy and hope that I was re-experiencing romantic rescue fantasies that had been forgotten long ago... The only problem was that, having got this man to fall in love with me, I had to *keep on* not being myself... I had deceived him by deceiving myself, and I'm still working on what I learned. But I do know that I chose an opposite as a dramatic example of what I missed in myself. (Steinem, *Revolution From Within*: 264–67)

Experts who write about romance, love or sex addiction agree that a heterosexual woman who continually seeks out one romantic encounter after another is looking for rescue in the form of male approval. She is looking for a man to rescue her from her own bad feelings about herself. Women who are serial sex, love or romance addicts feel almost frantic without male approval; it is in these situations where a woman can lose her selfhood; she de-selfs, as discussed earlier, adopting the man's needs or values as her own.

AFFAIRS

First, an affair, in the context of this discussion, means that a person already committed in a relationship is having another one on the sly. I am not referring to two single consenting adults. When the woman is single, and the man is married, I also discount this as an affair, for the purposes of this book.

Affairs are unhealthy when they are based in fantasy instead of reality, and when they are distractions from real life. When we don't want to feel the pain in our lives, we can wander into affairs that rescue us from that pain. Serial affairs (meaning, one after another instead of "once in a blue moon"), fall into the category of romance, sex or love addiction. These are affairs that can involve obsessions, which can take any form.

When affairs erupt once in a blue moon, the timing of that affair is significant, and the right question to ask is not why you are drawn to this person, but what is happening in your life right now that draws you to this person. A woman who is lonely may simply crave good company, but may be investing all kinds of extraordinary qualities on the person she is drawn to, to make it seem as though this incredible person fell from the sky into her life—as though it is the person, and not her life, that is the issue. The truth is usually less dramatic: she may be bored with her current partner, feeling disconnected or isolated, and the person that "fell into her life" just came at the right time, and does not deserve the unreal qualities she is projecting onto him. Often, the "good company" involves flirtation, compliments and validation—things she is not getting in her life from her current partner.

Affairs need not be sexual. They can be affairs of the heart or mind, which often take the form of obsessing for hours over someone you probably don't know very well; or spending hours on the Internet having a cybersex relationship with someone who may be spinning a completely fictitious self for your entertainment; or living for your next encounter with "the friend" you want to have sex with (but aren't), as Charlotte did:

> Mario was my professor; I was the 43-year-old cliché graduate student. Mario taught economics, and I was doing my MBA part-time. Mario was married; so was I, but we discussed how wonderful and freeing it was to just have a friendship with someone of the opposite sex. Mario was upfront about his attraction to me, but kept telling me that he did not believe in being unfaithful, and that he just didn't have the energy to leave his wife and family, even though he felt I was a beautiful and intelligent woman—a "nice package" he would say.

I wanted nothing more than to leave my husband for Mario. The truth is, no man had tempted me before as much as he did. I stopped living my life normally, and would just live for my "Mario" moments. I kept thinking I could live off the few hours a week I had of him during coffees, lunches and walks. It got to the point where all I did was long for him at the expense of everything else. My work suffered, and I had to quit the MBA program. I couldn't keep up. Mario didn't seem at all to be suffering from his "friendship" and my romance. Eventually, I had to cut the relationship off.

When affairs are sexual, they become unhealthy if you are living for your next sexual encounter, and are turning your life upside down in between. This usually means secrets and lies. One psychiatrist aptly said of affairs: it's not the sex, it's the secrets that destroy the trust, as Nancy reveals:

I became a very cool liar, even though my husband, in the past, could always tell when I was lying. Fred and I would communicate by cell phone only. My service was off for about a week, and I thought I would go crazy. I was paralyzed with the thought that Fred may have ended it; that I might not see him again. I kept telling my husband it was work and that I was just preoccupied. I slipped out to a pay phone and called Fred on his cell, like some cheap tramp; when we made arrangements to meet, I felt as though I could make it another week. All I had to do was live until Thursday, when I could have my fix.

Ultimately, very few affairs end with the famous "If you can paint, I can walk" line that makes us all feel good at the end of the film *An Affair To Remember*. Most affairs end badly. Someone wants more than the other person wants, which eventually leads someone to cutting off the affair. The pieces you're left with at the end of the affair are the building blocks to understanding why you went where you did for passion—or why you went where you did in order to "feel your life"—this book's definition of passion. If you can answer that question, you can usually start to create the conditions necessary for a more fulfilling life, or at least a life based in reality instead of fantasy.

In this chapter we see that when we unconsciously wander into crazy places for passion, our wandering sets off a series of events that can lead us toward self-actualization. These crazy places we find ourselves in can make us angry, but our anger is our warning signal that something is not acceptable. If we can actually be moved towards anger, and express it openly, we can be motivated and mobilized in a different, healthier direction.

6

CONSUMING PASSIONS
FOOD, DRINK AND OTHER ADDICTIONS

The French have a saying that is derived from the lyric of an old French torch song: *Regret nothing—in matters of love and food.* Puzzled scientists who have been trying to figure out why the French have such low rates of heart disease in spite of their diet of heavy cream sauces have found that the answer to the "French Paradox" is passion. The French are passionate about their food and really enjoy it. They "feel their food," so to speak. They never think of food as "sinful"; instead, they simply think of it as "tasty." To the French, food is a work of art, meant to be enjoyed. To the North American, food is "calories" and "fattening" and "forbidden."

North Americans tend to think about food as either fuel or poison; they fear the effect food will have on their bodies. In France, good food feeds the soul, not the body. (Apparently, General Charles de Gaulle used to say, "It's difficult to govern a country that has 500 varieties of cheese.") In France, the idea of "food police" watching every gram of fat is mocked. What is also mocked is the way in which North Americans eat: everywhere and anywhere is a dining room. We eat in our cars, while walking on the street, and at our desks when we work. In France, eating is at restaurants or at dinner tables. The North American pattern of eating is considered by the French to be nomadic eating, or vagabond feeding and grazing.

There is also a huge distinction between quantity and quality of food. In North America, we are taught that large portions are good, even if the food is mediocre. In France, the quality and taste of the food is the most important factor, and when taste is there, and the quality of the food is high, the appetite is satiated, and the quantity or portion size is not important. Ultimately, the French Paradox reveals a lot about North American women, food and passion. It is through the woman's body, in particular, that we see the results of the North American love-hate relationship with food, and it is the woman who uses her relationship with food to express the passions her culture denies her.

When women cannot fully express their feelings, or feel their lives in appropriate ways, many use food, alcohol or drugs as tools to enable feeling. Many women will substitute food for other things that are missing in their lives, such as sexual satisfaction, love or other sensuous aspects of life. When it comes to addiction (which can also include food), therapists who work with women and addiction have found that unlike men, women do not turn to drugs or alcohol to numb feeling, but to *enable* feeling. Many women only find their voice through drugs or alcohol. Women who have "de-selfed," and have not been able to express anger, will often use alcohol or drugs as a means of expressing anger.

On the flip side, when women feel their lives are out of control, or are not feeling their lives at all, they may use food as a way to regain control in their lives, or regain feeling, which is what is behind women manipulating their body sizes through food refusal or purging behaviours (for thin bodies), or overeating behaviours (for large bodies). This chapter is not about dieting; it looks at eating behaviours in the context of women and passion.

WOMEN, PASSION AND BODY SIZE

What does our body size say about our passions, or how we're feeling our lives? It is my theory that because our body sizes can be manipulated and changed through eating, dieting, starving, exercising and so on, the female body has become live sculpture for women, who are projecting their passions onto their bodies. Typically, what we are lacking on the inside shows on the outside. For example, when women are depressed, their body sizes frequently become smaller through loss of appetite. When women are coping with past trauma resulting from sexual abuse, their bodies often become larger to protect or hide the self, as well as to make the body less appealing to potential attackers.

So you see, there are just as many women who have an interest in being large as in being thin. By understanding how our passions are projected onto our body sizes, we may be able to understand our eating behaviours in more meaningful ways.

Being preoccupied with our body size is nothing new. As
mentioned earlier, even Eleanor Roosevelt struggled with it.
Eleanor grew up feeling unattractive, and although she
remains one of the most accomplished and fascinating
women in history, when asked if she had any regrets she
replied: "Just one. I wish I'd been prettier." Her mother was
beautiful and dainty; Eleanor felt shy, gawky, too tall and out
of place. To compensate for her size, she even forced her voice
to a higher register, which later was ridiculed by the press and
her critics.

Eleanor's marriage to her charming cousin, Franklin D.
Roosevelt, was largely a trade; Franklin appreciated Eleanor's
mind, but would find his sexual life elsewhere, which drove
Eleanor's passions into other areas, including relationships
with other women. What has recently surfaced about her life
is that biographers now believe she had an eating disorder.
The continuous sexual betrayals by her husband seemed to
fuel long episodes of food refusal or purging (it appears to
most that she was bulimic). But Eleanor's preoccupation with
her body size predated her marriage, and from her own words
in letters, interviews and autobiographical accounts, she most
likely began to control her body size to conform more to the
size of her own mother, as well as to the terribly confined role
women of her day were expected to play. Gloria Steinem has
this to say about Eleanor:

> Though she rose above these betrayals (Franklin's), her
> restricted upbringing, and her own shyness to become one
> of the most compassionate and humane leaders of her
> time—and though one hopes for her sake that she did have

the affairs with a man and perhaps a woman friend or two that her letters hint at—Eleanor Roosevelt's triumphant and world-respected later years were still haunted by an uncertain, unpretty girl of the past. (Steinem, *Revolution From Within*: 225–26)

A more recent example of a bulimic public female figure is the late former Princess of Wales, Diana, whose episodes of what she called "rampant bulimia—if there is such a thing..." compensated for her imprisoned existence, where she was unable to express any of her feelings. Diana described the food in her bingeing episodes as feeling like a "warm hug."

According to Gloria Steinem, rich cultures often prefer thin women and poor cultures fat ones because, as far as possessions go (and women are still possessions) whatever is rarest confers the most status. All patriarchal cultures idealize, sexualize and most often prefer weak women. Even strong women labourers often envy and even imitate the fragile, delicate look of wealthy women.

What it means to be thin

There are many socio-economic messages associated with a thin body. From the perspective of passion, a thin body sends the message of control. To be in control of our passions, our feelings, our emotions is something that is revered in our culture. A thin body is also feminine, which also implies a masculine emotional framework. A "successful" woman is a tall, thin, mannish woman who does not show evidence, on her body, of being female or of harbouring reproductive organs. The beauty standard that we see on fashion runways and in magazines reflects the masculinization of the female form.

In Western culture, we have come to associate feminine curves with loss of control. The successful woman can look like a man because she controls her food intake. Some experts add that the control of internal impulses such as hunger are perceived as the conquering of animal instincts. The unsuccessful woman cannot control her food intake and therefore takes on the rounder shape, which is rejected by our society. (This is often limited to the Western stereotype, however; other cultures have different beauty standards.) So now, controlling food is synonymous with self-control, self-discipline and ultimately, success—another facet of the power struggle.

For many women, controlling the shape of their bodies gives them a sense of accomplishment. The irony is that a thin body can leave the impression of frailty or even illness. Samantha's mixed feelings about her thinness confirm this:

> I was going through a very stressful divorce and had lost a considerable amount of weight. I was at a social function in the midst of it, and several people commented that I had lost weight. At first I felt good that people noticed, but when a lot of people asked about my health, I realized that the comments were out of concern rather than praise for my "accomplishment" of losing weight. One woman asked if I had been dieting on purpose, and I said, "It's the Divorce Diet." Still, I secretly loved being a size 4 again (prior to my divorce I was a 12).

What it means to be fat

The alarming sentiment "I'd rather be dead than fat" was expressed by many women interviewed in the acclaimed documentary on eating disorders *The Famine Within* (1991). From a passion perspective, the fat woman in Western culture is considered to be out of control. However, in other cultures, fat women are nurturers, sensuous and life-giving. The image of the fat woman as appealing and nurturing occasionally breaks through to Western women, as Stephanie tells us:

I have always battled with my weight, and am now a large woman. After the birth of my second child, I just couldn't lose my weight, and am continuously being reminded of it everywhere I go. I always resent assumptions that I am on a diet when I am not. I am just tired of fighting my form, and have decided to focus on other things in my life—like being a good mother to my children.

One day I was looking through some Caribbean travel brochures and came across a picture of a huge black woman, who had a wonderful smile on her face, surrounded by luscious fruits and delicious foods. I thought how wonderful it would be to be hugged by this woman. The image was obviously deliberate: this woman's size was conveying the "size" of the time we would have if we travelled to her country. A GREAT, BIG, WONDERFUL, LUSCIOUS, SENSUOUS, PASSIONATE time was all I could think of. I then asked my daughter one day how it felt to be hugged by me, and she said that she loved my "fat" and hoped that didn't hurt my feelings. It was the best compliment I ever got, and I hugged her with all my fat.

Feminist therapists maintain that being fat is perceived by many as a very public rebellion against the role many women are asked to play in society. Women are the ones who usually do the purchasing and preparing of food for the family. We are the nurturers and providers. At the same time, we are continuously being deluged with those impossible standards of beauty, fitness and thinness through media images. How do these conflicting images affect us? For many women, the effect is a feeling of powerlessness. And depending on the woman, manipulating body size to be bigger by eating food again expresses unconscious desires to achieve more control over our lives.

Therapists who work with women on weight loss issues observe that fat both isolates a woman and publicly proclaims her a failure. Women, of course, know this, and sometimes use it for psychological advantage. In other words, to the woman, the fat can excuse her from being successful in two specific areas: sexual and financial (career-related success). Many women fear being perceived on sexual terms by male colleagues, or have been so perceived in the past.

On the flip side, many women who have never had success in their lives, sexual or financial, use their fat as a way to remain isolated. This allows them to say to themselves: "If I were thin, I'd be successful." The fatness becomes the reason for failed attempts at personal success, which shields many women from facing their own inner demons and fears, keeping them from the successes they really want.

Perhaps one of the most powerful messages conveyed through fat is that the fat woman feeds herself in a world where she is not supposed to feed her desires in any straightforward way. By feeding herself, she is not selfless, but she is made to feel guilty about feeding herself. Josie comments:

> People are always commenting about what I choose to eat or put on my plate in the vein of concern. "We're only concerned about your health," they say. But no one seems to be concerned about the health of a woman who is thin. At least my bones won't break when I'm past menopause. I don't want to get into depriving myself of food; I think it's healthy to have an appetite and to want to feed yourself. Still, the looks I get when I put butter on my bread at a restaurant... You'd think I was snorting cocaine at the table or something.

For many women—especially women who have gained their weight after childbirth, fat has nothing to do with sexuality or personal/financial success. It has to do with their relationship with their mother, and their own feelings of nurturing and being a mother. After all, it is a mother's breasts that initially nurture us, and it is through our mothers that we learn about food and food behaviours. Our mothers are also the source of love, comfort, emotional support and sense of what is acceptable. Even when we do not get this from our own mothers, we still associate mothering with these behaviours.

Therapists have observed that body size and eating get tangled up in mother-daughter relationships, and can have varied meanings for the overweight woman. In other words, what your fat says to your mother can mean anything from: "I'm a big girl and can look after myself" to "I'm a mess and can't look after myself." Some daughters use fat to actually reject their mother's standards, or to express anger at their mothers for inadequate nurturing.

In other cases, the fat is an unconscious desire to incorporate your mother into your body because she's soothing and nurturing. It's a rather brilliant way of taking your mother with you wherever you go. When asked what she thinks of when the word "fat woman" is used, Abbie said:

> I think of being a child in my grandmother's arms. She had enormous—no—humungo—breasts, and I would fall asleep on them listening to her reading me a story. But I don't want to look like my grandmother. I had a breast reduction operation in my early 20s, and was reduced to a C-cup, which I feel is large enough, but not too large. I wonder if my grandmother, given the choice, would have reduced her size, even though it was her size that we actually loved. To me, a grandmother just isn't a grandmother if she isn't large, and huggable. And she didn't seem to be unhappy because of her size; she spread happiness around wherever she went. I miss her and dream of her sometimes. She did die young of a heart attack, I presume, because she was too fat.

Many women find their fat expresses anger at the beauty standard and the restrictive sexual role they're asked to play.

The fat is not protection but a deliberate attempt to offend the world. Here, the fat says to the world: "Screw you! If you *really* want to get to know me, you'll take the time to penetrate my layers. Otherwise, *I* don't want to know you!" Claudine shares this about herself and her weight:

> I'm a very funny—as in ha-ha—person. But there's always a hesitation with people (men, especially) when I first meet them. The men usually look me over. They look at my face, then my tits (and probably my ass, which is big, when I turn around). Then I say something that makes them laugh and they look at me like a human being. I use my humour to welcome people into my body. I am not "funny" because I'm fat; I'm just funny, and *happen* to be fat.

Susie Orbach, author of *Fat Is a Feminist Issue,* reports what women say their fat means to them:

- To be fat means to get into the subway and worry about whether you can fit into the allotted space.

- To be fat means to compare yourself to every other woman, looking for the ones whose own fat can make you relax.

- To be fat means to be outgoing and jovial to make up for what you think are your deficiencies.

- To be fat means to refuse invitations to go to the beach or dancing.

- To be fat means to be excluded from contemporary mass culture, from fashion, sports and the outdoor life.

- To be fat is to be a constant embarrassment to yourself and your friends.

- To be fat is to worry every time a camera is in view.

- To be fat means to feel ashamed for existing.

- To be fat means having to wait until you are thin to live.

- To be fat means to have no needs.

- To be fat means to be constantly trying to lose weight.

- To be fat means to take care of others' needs.

- To be fat means to wait for the man who will love you despite the fat—the man who will fight through the layers.

- Above all, the fat woman wants to hide. Paradoxically, her lot in life is to be perpetually noticed.

USING FOOD TO CONTROL PASSIONS

Whether women are thin or fat, they often use food to control their passions, meaning, they may feel their lives through overindulging in food, or they may feel their lives through depriving themselves of food. In the first case, women may simply eat a lot of food, particularly foods that give them comfort, such as foods with fatty textures—foods that are "rich," "creamy" or "soft" are typical comfort foods that fulfill emotions rather than appetite.

Some women feel so much guilt over indulging and enjoying food, they develop complex bingeing/purging behaviours, known as bulimia nervosa ("hunger like an ox due to mental disorder"). Those women purge after a bingeing episode by inducing vomiting, abusing laxatives and diuretics or by overexercising. Francine shares her experiences with bulimia:

I have only vague memories of eating a meal and allowing myself to be "filled up"—you know—that feeling of warmth and satisfaction after a good meal. Sometimes I wish I could get it back, but I can't allow myself that satisfaction. One day in particular stands out in my mind. I wandered into a bakery after a very stressful day and saw this huge birthday cake. I wanted it, but I was too ashamed to buy it for myself. I told the baker it was for my mother, and waited while they wrote on the cake "Happy Birthday [Mom]." They carefully wrapped it in a box for me. I took it home and consumed the entire cake in about an hour. Then I began to panic. "What have I done?" I kept asking myself. I made myself "do the deed" but I had to throw up several times that night to feel as though the cake was no longer a part of me. How I could want something that large and sinful to go inside me in the first place was a terrifying reality to face; but getting it out consumed more energy than I had.

I was so drained and exhausted from the vomiting, I felt I should eat something, but I didn't want to destroy all my hard work and effort. I was so tired, I thought maybe just some vegetables. Then I had to have dip and vegetables. Then, chips, dip and vegetables. Then I made pasta, and the cooking and eating went on all night. I called in sick the next morning so I could get everything I ate out of me. My eating and vomiting actually consumed my time and my life for years. I came to realize much later that the binge/purge pattern I had developed was my way of avoiding life. As sick as it was, it was safer to occupy my time with my bulimia than go out into the world.

This narrative, from Cathy, appears in the book *Women's Conflicts About Eating and Sexuality*:

I used to binge about once a week. Then it gradually increased to the point where I would do this every day. If I was at home and not working, I would binge and throw up several times a day. A few times I tried to stop the crazy behavior, but it was out of my control. Around this time, I also got a job as an airline stewardess and had to be weighed all the time to meet their requirements. That just seemed to feed into what I was doing to myself. Now I am obsessed with food. All I can think of day and night is what I'm going to eat next. Visions of cookies and chocolate eclairs appear in front of me as I am trying to do my work, as I talk to people. No matter what I am doing, I am always planning my next binge. (Meadow and Weiss: 16).

Women may also become martyrs in their refusal of food, feeling their lives through the suffering that comes with starvation. This eating behaviour is known as anorexia nervosa ("loss of appetite due to mental disorder"). Colleen, a recovering anorexic, says:

> One of the more twisted things I would do when I was starving myself would be to make a fabulous meal for my friends, and not eat a bite of anything myself. I would feel powerful when they would ooh and aah about how delicious my food was, yet see that I was not eating it myself. In fact, I used to get a rush from my own hunger pangs. The more intense the hunger, the more powerful I felt. It was like I was addicted to the rush of my own self-control. I felt superior; as though very few women could actually do what I do. Now that I am eating, though, I feel envy at how other people can enjoy their food; I can eat, but I can't allow myself to really enjoy it.

What are women controlling?

When women control their food intake through starvation or purging, they are controlling their feelings—both negative and positive. In some cases, the food can even become an outlet for anger, as Emily reveals:

> I had a fight with my mother over the usual: my life! She disapproved of yet another choice I'd made. We were having about 20 people for dinner (it was around the holidays), and she had baked a couple of loaves of bread. I grabbed one of the loaves and just tore into it with my teeth,

feeling as though I was hurting her. Even though I didn't even want the bread, or enjoy it, I ate the whole loaf. The biting and chewing of something my mother wanted to show off to her company gave me pleasure. When I went home, I threw up.

Research on bulimia and anorexia reveals that women with these eating disorders are usually overachievers in other aspects of their lives, and view excess weight as an announcement to the world that they are out of control. This view becomes more distorted as time goes on, until the act of eating food in public (in bulimia) or at all (in anorexia) is perceived to be equivalent to a loss of control.

In anorexia, the person's emotional and sensual desires are channelled through food. These desires are so great that the anorexic fears that once she eats she'll never stop, since her appetite/desires will know no natural boundaries; the fear of food drives the disease. Many experts also see this eating disorder as an addiction to perfection; the sense of control the eating-disordered woman gains through this behaviour is the drug.

Most of us find it easier to relate to the bulimic than the anorexic; bulimics express their loss of control through bingeing. Bulimics then purge to regain their control. There is a feeling of comfort for bulimics in both the binge and the purge. Bulimics are sometimes referred to as "failed anorexics" because they'd starve if they could. Anorexics, however, are masters of control. They never break.

Since the onset of anorexia is typically during adolescence, when the female body is changing dramatically, the traditional view was that a young woman was trying to stop her body from changing into a woman, which has many meanings in the context of passion. By forcing the body to stop growing, the young woman is trying to stop her progression into a sexual being; she is also (unconsciously) stopping her inevitable progression towards her death. The irony is that she is nearing her death faster by starving her body.

Many writers on the subject of anorexia point to the connection between starving and feeling; it is through the pain of starvation that women feel their lives, which brings us back to the discussion of suffering in chapter 1. Jungian analyst and author Marion Woodman, in her book on eating disorders, *The Owl Was a Baker's Daughter*, quotes a client:

> I only know that when I hoped, I was thin; when I was in despair, I was fat... I eat and gain weight and I don't feel the tensions anymore. Now I am fat, but not content. I find myself wishing for the pain of dieting again, the agony of spirit, because in that state I feel I am growing. I feel guilty in this dead, fat state. There must be some way of being both thin and without the agony of too much awareness. It is sick to wish the suffering to come back just so I can feel alive. (Woodman: 57)

Other authors emphasize that there is a communication pattern that is distinct in the families of anorexic women. The family is usually very vocal, and its members share their ideas and feelings, but when the anorexic girl tries to join in discussions, she is dismissed. She is often a "shadow woman" growing up in the shadow of other high-achieving family members. Control of her food intake becomes a weapon she uses to assert her individuality. She finds perfection through her starvation, or fasting. Woodman suggests that fasting actually heightens the senses.

There is also a mother-daughter drama that is played out in anorexic women. The control of the desires is a way to harness control over the precariousness of life itself, which the mother has become an expert at controlling, but the daughter fears she cannot.

EATING AND SEXUALITY

Equating food with sex is nothing new. The Hausa of Nigeria, for example, use the same word—*ci* (pronounced "chi")—for both "eating" and "sex." In the Mexican film *Like Water For Chocolate* (the title refers to the boiling temperature water needs to be for hot chocolate), the heroine, a wonderful cook, who is prevented from marrying her true love (he is married to her sister), makes love to him through her cooking. In a beautiful scene, in which she prepares a poultry dish in rose petal sauce, all of her desires get mixed into the sauce, which ignites the passions of all who consume it.

According to Marion Woodman, both the obese women and the bulimic woman invests all of her hungers—sexual and spiritual—into food. In one sense, she can even make her desires vanish through food, which is a similar pattern seen in women and alcohol and women who "de-self."

As for the anorexic woman, she is the "nutritional virgin." In the past, women exhibited starving, bingeing/purging behaviours when it came to sex. The "sexual anorexic" was the virgin who denied herself sexual desires, but at the same time was preoccupied with them. The "sexual bulimic" was the "slut" who slept around, and was made to feel very guilty about indulging her desires; she may have even purged the consequences through a coat-hanger abortion. Now that sexuality is allowed, however, the battle of desires is fought not in the back seat of a convertible, but in the kitchen.

In the past, young girls learned to repress their sexual appetites because of the consequences (pregnancy, becoming unmarriageable); today, young girls learn to repress their appetites because they fear similar social consequences. Similarities between the forbidden pleasures of sex in the 1950s and 1960s (through romance novels or movies) are similar in scope to the forbidden pleasures of food we see played out in ads. When you look at the advertising surrounding certain desserts or chocolate, the image of a woman alone, having an orgasmic experience with her chocolate, is playing to these fantasies.

Some authors have noted that women today are as obsessed with food as their mothers (or grandmothers) were with sex. It's the same problem with a different variable; we are still looking at women obsessed with controlling their passions. Fat on the bodies of women is as shameful as the "A" sewn onto the clothing of an adulterous woman, as depicted in the nineteenth-century novel *The Scarlet Letter*. The fat marks her as someone who has let her desires overtake her. The lines between sex and food are so blurry, women in the midst of a sexual encounter are still thinking about food, as Cathy, from *Women's Conflicts About Eating and Sexuality*, shares:

Two years ago I got a new job. I also met a wonderful man. We started seeing each other regularly and fell in love to the point that we decided to get married. At that time I thought to myself, "Well, now you have it all again, you don't need to binge all the time anymore."… I really thought that if everything went okay in my life again, I would stop being so obsessed with food. But I still am, and I can't understand it. Tom and I got married two weeks ago. We went on this wonderful romantic honeymoon, and even while we were making love, all I could think of was when would we stop so that I could eat. While he was touching me, all I could picture were images of food. I am so obsessed with it, I don't know what to do. I've heard it said men lust for women, and women lust for food. I never realized how true that was—or how pathetic. (Meadow and Weiss: 16)

The spirit and the flesh

Whether it's food or sex, women have been trying to control their flesh through their spirit for centuries. Throughout history, women have continuously bounced between abstaining and indulging, or fulfilling and depriving. In fact, of the 42 women in Italy who were called saints in the fourteenth century, half exhibited anorexic behaviour; using the will to conquer our fleshly passions is considered saintly. Women self-mutilate when it comes to matters of both sex and food. Whether it's starvation, self-induced vomiting, stomach stapling or jaw wiring, or alternatively, piercing the vulva or nipples, or staying in abusive sexual relationships, the pleasures of the flesh cannot be indulged without tremendous remorse for many women.

By starving themselves, women can also make their flesh disappear. When they are thin, and have no flesh, the twisted perception is that they can stop their feelings and desires. By having a body, they feel their lives—hunger and desire (for food or sex), fullness and frustration, pleasure and pain. But when they are a flat figure—an image instead of a body—or the "no-body body," the desires vanish.

Women tend to find it safer to live outside their bodies than inside. Research consistently shows, for example, that young women are far more concerned with how people see their bodies than what *they* are seeing from *within* their bodies. Many girls and women talk about how their feelings make them look, rather than how they make them feel. In essence, the current beauty standard denies women their active desires. Women learn very early to deny "embodied passion." Women grow up believing that they are more desirable when they are an image instead of a real body. Indeed, by flattening themselves into two dimensions, there is a flattening of all bodily desires.

BOTTLE AND SUBSTANCE

When you look at all of the academic articles on women and alcohol abuse, the one common fact you'll find is this: women drink for completely different reasons than men, and the Alcoholics Anonymous 12-step programs are usually not successful ways for women to stop drinking. These programs were modelled after male patterns of alcoholism. Women who drink come from a range of educational and economic back-grounds, too. Highly educated women are just as likely to have a drinking problem as women with less education.

From the perspective of women and passion, women typi-cally use alcohol to free their inhibitions and enable their passions and feelings to escape. Many cannot function sexu-ally without drinking first to loosen up. They use the bottle to come *out* of the bottle. Men, however, tend to use alcohol to numb their feelings. Women are more likely to drink wine rather than hard liquor, while men tend to use the hard stuff to get drunk fast.

Women can be incredibly passionate about their wine, as Grace reveals:

> I need my wine every night. Not a whole bottle—just two or three glasses a night. If you want to label me an alcoholic then I would counter with the term "highly functional alco-holic." It doesn't interfere with my life, it's just something I really enjoy, look forward to, and need to have waiting when I come home. My boyfriend doesn't join me when I drink; he judges me, and he will often voice his disap-proval. One day I said to him, "You know what...? I'll replace *you* before I replace my wine!"

For the most part, you'll read different statistics about the woman alcoholic. She may have a "dependent" personality, be more likely to suffer from depression, or come from a family of alcoholics. For the most accurate take on women and alcohol, go to your local video store. Most of what you need to know about women and drinking you'll find captured on film, in movies such as *The Days of Wine and Roses,* starring Jack Lemmon and Lee Remick. The woman in *Days* is very passive and sweet; she tells her alcoholic boyfriend that she prefers chocolate to alcohol. So he introduces her into his world through the liqueur crème de cacao. She likes it very much; she finds a new voice through the alcohol. She becomes witty and sexual. And so it goes until their lives become destroyed by their addiction. And true to life, he finds salvation through AA; she, on the other hand, does not like the format of AA. She doesn't benefit from it in the same way he does. In the end, he is saved and must accept that only she can save herself if she chooses.

For another true-to-life portrayal, slip *Who's Afraid of Virginia Woolf?* into your VCR and watch Elizabeth Taylor and Richard Burton imitate their lives through their art in the film version of Edward Albee's celebrated play. Both Martha and George are alcoholics. George uses alcohol to numb his voice and feelings—to forget the past; Martha, on the other hand, uses alcohol to enable herself to voice her frustrations with the past. She blurts out to their guests one terrible truth after another about George, their life, and ultimately, all of her lost dreams. We learn, for example, that she is the daughter of a famous professor; she is actually brighter than George, and had she been given an opportunity, could have become as brilliant as her father. Instead, she married George, a mediocre academic who secured a position with the university through Martha's father. An old story. And so true.

The bottom line is that the social triggers for alcoholism in women are no different than for anything else discussed in this book. By being forced to play a continuous, subservient role in our culture, where their passions are not allowed, women's responses and coping skills to survive this role come out in various ways. Fay reveals the core truth behind women's drinking:

> I am a teacher and my husband is an engineer; the company gatherings I'm forced to go to are dreadfully dull, and so to survive them, I usually get pleasantly pissed. My husband tells me I'm "too loud" when I drink. But surely I'm no louder than some of the clods I have to talk to. A couple of glasses of wine or even beer just makes me feel sort of loosy-goosy. It's just enough to make me feel at ease to joke, tease, rib people... you know. But sometimes I blurt things out I would never say normally. I actually said to my husband's boss that I would be "much finer if you turned down the stress level at that sweatshop you're running" when he said to me, "Hi there... you're looking mighty fine tonight!" In fact, the boss wasn't offended and thought my comment was funny, but my husband was mortified for days after that and forbid me to drink again.

And so the drinking pattern starts. Usually it feels good as an enabler, but because alcohol is, in fact, addictive, it turns into an addiction. Creative women often use alcohol as a creative enabler, which is why so many women artists have struggled with alcoholism. Alcoholism and depression often go hand in hand, but it is more accurate to say that the depression usually comes first, and the alcohol is the temporary rescue from the depression. Many women also silently drink, which enables freer thinking, relaxation and a time for them to let down their guard.

When women become addicted to alcohol, they may become what's known as cross-addicted, combining alcohol with other substances, such as various prescription or illegal drugs. But the reasons for substance abuse or substance addiction are the same: they are enablers. One of the emerging patterns in research on women and addiction is that women will also seek out pleasure drugs, such as cocaine. The drug heightens their pleasures, and for a lot of women the drug offers them their first completely selfish, indulgent experience with pleasure. It is something they do that is just for them. When women are denied permission to pleasure themselves, drugs can become their pleasure enabler.

In this chapter, we see how food, alcohol or other substances can be used when women's feelings and passions are bottled up, denied or have no place to go. The tremendous energy that is usurped through continuous obsessing over food and other addictions can be channelled in more positive ways. In fact, therapists who specialize in women and eating disorders find that the path to recovery lies in mourning for the loss of the "dream body" and accepting the real body, the real person. When the body becomes the woman's enemy, only when she reclaims the body for herself can she really begin to feel her flesh, and her life. Women recovering from eating disorders and addiction have repeatedly expressed surprise at how much energy they now realize was consumed by their disordered food habits or addiction.

Energy can often be expended in more proactive and creative ways, as we see in the next chapter.

7

CREATIVE PASSIONS
WOMEN AND CREATIVITY

Self-expression is a passionate act. When women express their feelings through their work, art (by this, I mean art in all its forms: words, fine arts, visual arts, healing arts, performing arts), hobbies or sport, they are not only feeling their lives but *expressing their lives.*

Women have had to suffer for the sake of their creativity in different ways than men. Until this century, women were not encouraged to be creative, and many were forced to hide their art, or to write or create under male pseudonyms such as the nineteenth-century English novelist George Eliot (author of *Silas Marner* among a host of books), whose real name was Mary Ann Evans.

For many women, their creativity is the only outlet for their passions. This chapter not only looks at how women express their passions through their work, art or sport, but also at other creative ways women use to feel their lives, or express their passion. Creativity is a big topic; this chapter examines only a few creative forms to tell a universal tale. A sentiment expressed by a character in an Ingmar Bergman film captures what many creative women (and men) have felt: "I could always live in my art, but never in my life."

WOMEN OUTSIDE THE BOX

I define creativity as simply thinking "outside the box." Historically, when women thought outside their traditional roles, they were often diagnosed as hysteric, or declared mad and imprisoned in madhouses, as discussed earlier. The practice of confining "thinking" women to madhouses became so widespread that Daniel Defoe criticized it in 1687, calling attention to the "vile practice now so much in vogue among the better sort, as they were called, but the worst sort, in fact, namely the sending of their wives to madhouses at every whim or dislike."

One of the most famous cases of involuntary confinement involved Elizabeth Packard, whose husband committed her to an asylum in 1860 because she dared to question religion. Elizabeth was kidnapped by her husband, who then withheld her children, income from her inheritance, clothes, books and other possessions. Packard began a diary of asylum events (or, rather, horrors), and never referred to it as a hospital, but always as a prison. It is Packard who first makes the analogy of institutional psychiatry and the Inquisition.

Other definitions of creativity assert that it involves any kind of expression where you are either imposing your personal view of reality on the world or questioning conventional views; this takes courage, for when we risk disclosing our view of the world, we also risk ridicule and public ostracization.

Creativity, it has been shown, tends to spring from a deep need to express the true self, rather than for the sake of reward. Author Jean Baker Miller, who wrote about the psychology of women in the 1970s noted:

For women to act and react out of their own being is to fly in the face of their appointed definition and their prescribed way of living. To move toward authenticity also involves creation, in an immediate and pressing personal way. (Woodman: 120)

One of the most compelling examples of "outside the box" female thinkers can be seen in the surviving work of the lesser-known Charlotte Perkins Gilman (whose great-aunt was Harriet Beecher Stowe, author of *Uncle Tom's Cabin*). Gilman is best known for a daring short story called "The Yellow Wallpaper," first published in 1892 in the *New England Magazine*, which made headlines in its day, causing Gilman to respond with the essay "Why I Wrote 'The Yellow Wallpaper.'" The story fell into relative obscurity until it was reprinted in a feminist literary anthology in 1973.

The story documents Gilman's struggle with depression, which she openly admitted was caused by her limited role in society, and the ineffective "rest cure" that was prescribed by prominent American neurologist S. Weir Mitchell. The rest cure was to confine women to their rooms and deprive them of all intellectual stimulation, because it was believed that their illness (called then hysteria, and today, depression) was due to "overuse of the mind." It was believed that because women had inferior minds, overuse of them was unhealthy. No visitors were permitted. Only food and fresh air, and rest were the "cure"—which in fact drove women to the brink of madness. Mitchell actually advised Gilman to "live as domestic a life as possible... and never to touch pen, brush or pencil again as long she lived." Fortunately, Gilman did not take his advice.

Gilman's story is told in the first person, and focuses on a wallpaper pattern that the protagonist is forced to look at day and night while she is "resting." The story is filled with asides and commentary about the restrictions placed on creative outlets for women. One passage reads: "I don't know why I should write this, but I *must* say what I feel and think in some way—it is such a relief!" (Shulman, *The Yellow Wallpaper and Other Stories*: 10). The pattern on the wall that disturbs her so is a metaphor for the social patterns she found disturbing.

In her story Gilman actually denounced the rest cure, and cited Mitchell by name; she wrote the story with the express purpose of showing Dr. Mitchell the "error of his ways" in prescribing such a cure. The story raises still-relevant questions about how depression in women is treated, and also focuses on the fact that her illness is not "believed" by the protagonist's physician-husband, something that as a bioethicist, I can tell you is just as much a problem for twenty-first century women as it was for nineteenth-century women.

It is through Gilman's creativity that she was able not only to save herself from her depressions (which recurred throughout her life), but also to emerge as a major voice of protest in the treatment of depression in women. She spent her life writing and lecturing extensively on how she felt women's roles ought to be changed. She was so ahead of her time, in fact, that she wrote extensively in her own midlife about "the woman of 50," questioning what they were supposed to do for the next 30 years of their lives when all the house chores were done. She also arranged for her own mercy killing (now called euthanasia) when she was diagnosed with breast cancer in 1934.

Gilman denounced convention, and refused to marry Walter Stetson, a painter related to the Stetson-hat family. She wrote Stetson:

> I cannot marry, although I am fitted to enjoy all that marriage can give to the utmost [she is referring here to sex]. Were I to marry, my thoughts, my acts, my whole life would be centred in husband and children. To do the work that I have planned I must be free. (Shulman, *The Yellow Wallpaper and Other Stories*: x)

Eventually, however, due to circumstances beyond her control, Gilman did marry Stetson, and wound up supporting his art and forsaking her own, a common pattern amongst creative women. Stetson, whose diaries and letters have also survived, wrote:

> One sees little just now of the daring and independent manner of the Charlotte that I first knew... she has tamed her effort to doing things for me and that has had a strange effect on her [he is referring to her "de-selfing"]. It has made her more like what is best in other women—more thoughtful, bland, gracious, humble, dependent. (Shulman, *The Yellow Wallpaper and Other Stories*: x)

Gilman wrote in her diary around this time: "I have lost *power*. I do not feel myself so strong a person as I was before. I seem to have taken a lower seat, to have become less in some way, to have shrunk." Gilman regained her power by ending her marriage. She later remarried a man who supported her writing and lecturing career. Gilman used her creativity to effect social change. She even said of her first collection of poems: "I don't call it a book of poems; I call it a tool box. It was written to drive nails with."

The connection between creativity and madness was made in chapter 4, where I discuss the undeniable fact that many creative women struggle with severe mood swings and manic depression. Unfortunately, the experience of being female is difficult enough; factor in the experience of being an artist and female, and life can become even more difficult. Celebrated author Margaret Atwood commented:

> By the time I got round to actually being a writer [she was speaking of 1964], I began to notice that women with vocations were considered rather odd, that biographies of famous women tended to point out how warped and/or sexually stunted or childless they were... but it was too late by then. I could see the disadvantages of being a woman, but somehow they didn't impress me as fatal or final... For a while there, you were made to feel that, if you were a poet and female, you could not really be serious about it unless you made at least one suicide attempt. So I felt I was running out of time. (Sullivan, *The Red Shoes*: 159)

WOMEN, PASSION AND THE DIARY

For many women, the diary is the recipient of their passions. In their diaries, they reveal their true feelings about their lives, and are able to actually feel their lives on paper. Through writing and journaling, millions of women find an outlet for their passions and desires each day.

Out of perhaps the most famous diary in history comes the powerful voice of young Anne Frank, the Jewish girl who hid with two other families in the "secret annex" during the Nazi occupation of Holland during the Second World War. Here she expresses her creative passions at the tender age of 13:

> I want to write, but more than that, I want to bring out all kinds of things that lie buried deep in my heart... I can shake off everything if I write; my sorrows disappear, my courage is reborn. But, and this is the great question, will I ever be able to write anything great, will I ever become a journalist or writer? I hope so, oh, I hope so very much, for I can recapture everything when I write, my thoughts, my ideals and my fantasies... So I go on again with fresh courage; I think I shall succeed, because I want to write! (Smith, *Women Who Write*: 45).

What continues to fascinate the world about *The Diary of Anne Frank*, which has been translated into virtually all written languages, is that it shows us how our creativity can save us, even in the face of overwhelming, impossible odds. Her diary also reveals the power of creative expression; when women express themselves in their own words, they give themselves voice, which gives their lives and experiences meaning. Although Anne did not survive the war (she died of typhoid in 1945, in the concentration camp Bergen-Belsen), her passions and her voice survived because she dared to express herself. Anne Frank never intended for her diary to be published; but her universal need to communicate on paper is felt by women everywhere, including Nina:

> In 1974, I was 33, divorced, broke and unskilled for the workforce. A friend encouraged me to take a creative-writing class, which was free through a community college, and throughout the various assignments, we were expected to begin a journal. Good writing, we were told, begins with journaling, where we record our thoughts, fears and so forth. The journals were not to be handed in, so many students in the class didn't bother with it. But I tried it. Once I started journaling, I found it was very therapeutic. I was able to articulate and organize my thoughts in ways that were not possible before. And because the journal was just for me, I found I was able to experiment with poetry, dialogue, stories and even a couple of really bad songs.
>
> Now that I'm older, I spend hours looking back on old journal entries. It's like going back in time; all the feelings and memories, some bad, some not so bad, are there for me to reflect on in my menopausal years! But through my journals I witness how much I've grown, because I've been through so much since that first day in that little class.
>
> I'm a lousy picture-taker, and still can't figure out my camcorder. So my journals remain as a written record of my life, which I hope someday I can leave to my children, who are now grown with their own families. My journal saved me from many a sleepless and lonely night, when I felt I

couldn't go on. My big project is to try to scan the entries into my computer, so I can print them like a book.

Journal writing is such a powerful tool for women, it has become a standard method of teaching writing and essay skills in virtually all institutions of higher learning. A few years ago, Oprah Winfrey used her influence to get women to begin writing a journal or diary because of the powerful effects it can have on enabling women who are otherwise without voice or expression. Using her own creativity to enable other women, she has resold the idea of journaling in an age where few people take the time to sit down and be still with their thoughts.

Oprah has taken journaling one step further by encouraging women to begin "gratitude journaling," where they think about what, in their lives, they are thankful for, and actually write it down. A firm believer in literacy, Oprah's influence on the comeback of journals can also enable many women who, in the past, might have been afraid to write because of their education levels, to find the courage to write and express themselves. For women who do not feel they are creative or artistic, journaling is an opportunity to express their feelings and passions.

The diary or journal style has also been employed by several authors as a literary technique. Alice Walker's *The Colour Purple* is a story of a poor, uneducated African-American woman, told in the diary style. Complete with misspelled words and poor grammar, the character in Walker's *Purple* shines through, demonstrating that communicating feelings on paper has nothing to do with education or grammatically correct writing. Renowned writer and poet Maya Angelou recalled in one broadcast interview that as a result of sexual abuse trauma, she was mute for many years. It was only through writing that she had a voice until she found her vocal voice again.

Another stellar example of the power of journal writing comes from Helen Keller, the writer and lecturer, blind and deaf at age 19 months, who literally felt her life with her fingers. In her autobiography, *The Story of My Life*, published in 1902, when she was 22, and dedicated to her close friend, Alexander Graham Bell, she writes:

> People who think that all sensations reach us through the eye and the ear have expressed surprise that I should notice any difference, except possibly the absence of pavements, between walking in city streets and in country roads. They forget that my whole body is alive to the conditions about me. The rumble and roar of the city smite the nerves of my face, and I feel the ceaseless tramp of an unseen multitude, and the dissonant tumult frets my spirit... I derive genuine pleasure from touching great works of art. As my finger tips trace line and curve, they discover the thought and emotion which the artist has portrayed. I can feel in the faces of gods and heroes hate, courage and love, just as I can detect them in living faces I am permitted to touch... The hands of those I meet are dumbly eloquent to me. The touch of some hands is an impertinence. I have met people so empty of joy, that when I clasped their frosty finger tips, it seemed as if I were shaking hands with a northeast storm. Others there are

whose hands have sunbeams in them, so that their grasp warms my heart. (Keller: 91, 96, 98)

In 1933, *the Atlantic Monthly* published Keller's article "Three Days to See," which served as an inspiration to America in the grip of the Depression. In her fantasies about what she would see, she was able to inspire her readers to take more pleasure in their surroundings:

I who am blind can give one hint to those who see—one admonition to those who would make full use of the gift of sight: Use your eyes as if tomorrow you would be stricken blind. Hear the music of voices, the song of a bird, the mighty strains of an orchestra, as if you would be stricken deaf tomorrow. Touch each object you want to touch as if tomorrow your tactile sense would fail. (Hermann, *Helen Keller*: 275)

The writer of those words was more in touch with her senses than most fully seeing and hearing women. An interesting note on Helen Keller is that though she was renowned for her brilliance in overcoming her disabilities, she was not permitted to marry in her day because of her disabilities. This was a great irony as she was very beautiful, and actually known for her voluptuous figure, angelic face and stunning blue eyes (which were later replaced with glass). Her hair was a fantastic shining mane of auburn. She once commented bitterly: "If I could see, I would marry first of all." Dorothy Hermann, her biographer, writes:

Beautiful, intelligent, high-strung and passionate. Helen might have lived the life of a spoiled, wilful, and highly sexed woman had the nature of her disability and her dependency on Annie Sullivan forced her into an entirely different existence, one in which she had to subjugate her own personal happiness as a female for the good of people afflicted like herself and other minorities. (Hermann, *Helen Keller*: xvi)

Helen Keller's interest in men was apparent, too. She wrote (perhaps in her ripening):

Masculine exhalations are, as a rule, stronger, more vivid, more widely differentiated than those of women. In the odor of young men there is something elemental, as of fire, storm and salt sea. It pulsates with buoyancy and desire. It suggests all the things strong and beautiful and joyous and gives me a sense of physical happiness. (Hermann, *Helen Keller*: 161)

Journal writing is also a branch of art therapy, and used as a tool by many therapists to get women to express feelings associated with deep trauma from childhood, particularly women who have suffered sexual abuse. Patricia found this a valuable asset in her own therapy:

When I began therapy several years ago, I actually couldn't express why I was there. My life just wasn't "working." I had been troubled by nightmares, and began to have flashes of very disturbing memories, but everything was fragmented. My life was fragmented into my work and then my total isolation at home. I had no friends, and was not in contact with my family. When I began to recover some memory of the abuse I suffered, I entered this blocked period where I couldn't talk at all. I almost felt it was not worth going to therapy and considered ending it. But my therapist gave me a piece of paper and a pen and said, "If you can't speak, write. Just get it out." I wrote one word on the page: "STOP." My therapist took the page and wrote: "Who?" I wrote: "Him." She wrote: "Who?" and through this process, which lasted over the course of a few sessions, I wrote, one day, the name of my stepbrother, who was the perpetrator of the abuse. I actually was able to remember "who" on paper, but not when I had to speak.

Women, letters and e-mails

Many women find self-expression through letters and e-mails to others. Women will often voice their feelings about their loves and lives to others on paper, even though they may be reluctant to keep a journal or diary.

Jane Goodall, one of the world's most celebrated zoologists, who devoted her life to the study of chimpanzees, and who has seen and learned more about chimps than any human being before her, lived in isolated terrain, and clearly used letter writing as an outlet for her feelings and passions. Goodall was passionate about her work, and tried to keep romantic entanglements from destroying her relationship with her true loves: her chimps. She wrote the following in a letter in 1956, when she was 22:

I have decided, even more firmly than when I spoke to you on the phone, that [her suitor] is no husband for me... If you want to know any reasons for my never marrying him I can let you have a string—e.g's television, too settled, too fond of creature comforts, doesn't like books etc., doesn't stand up straight, too fat, not handsome—but it goes down to the fact that I just don't love him one bit, so that's that—AND he knows it." (Peterson, *Africa in my Blood*: 72)

To her mother, she explains her feelings about another man:

Now, one little remonstration to you, Ma. You can't have understood me properly over one thing re. Brian. You say that (a) I don't go out with other men because B wouldn't like it, (b) why don't I try peeling layers off what I call 'stuffy' young men. Well, (a) I am sure I said at the present I have no desire to go out with anyone else, except occasionally, & therefore I am NOT unnecessarily giving up my freedom of personality... It is, without exception, so far they who try & do the peeling. I'm sure I've told you that all the young men out here have only one idea—to go to bed with one. (Peterson, *Africa in my Blood*: 135)

A protégé of the famous archaeologist and anthropologist Louis Leakey, who gave Goodall her start in Africa (he sent her to the Gombe Stream Chimpanzee Reserve on Lake Tanganyika, where she made her career), Leakey apparently wanted a romantic relationship with Goodall. She wrote:

> My situation here is really getting more and more tricky every day. Old Louis really is infantile in his infatuation and is suggesting the most impossible things. I have absolutely no intention of getting involved with him in the ways he suggests. (Peterson, *Africa in my Blood*: 118)

But Goodall was not uninterested in sex, as this letter to her mother demonstrates:

> I must tell you one other thing. I have found a most romantic lover. Every night he wakes me up, very gently, at about 2.30. He then creeps into my bed and makes love to me until I want to go to sleep again. (Peterson, *Africa in my Blood*: 91)

Passionate about her career and her work, she describes putting the National Geographic's Society's Committee for Research and Exploration chair, Dr. Leonard Carmichael, in his place through this letter excerpt:

> And he kept saying that when I was writing a scientific paper or my thesis I should say this or this, and not that or that. Until, in exasperation I said that I wasn't writing a thesis, but talking to him. And do you know, from that moment onwards, he was a changed man. (Peterson, *Africa in my Blood*: 342)

The deepest, most guarded passions of Eleanor Roosevelt were revealed in two sentences she wrote to the man she truly loved. His name was Dr. David Gurewitsch, a friend and physician, and son of Russian émigés. In Eleanor's later years, he was her companion. They had a deep friendship and love for one another, although the relationship was never sexual. Eleanor, well into her sixties, was heartbroken over the 20-year age difference between herself and this man she loved. Whenever I read these words, I have to admit I get choked up. To David she wrote: "What I have in the few years I have left is yours. My whole heart is yours."

THE CREATIVE RESCUE

The theme of rescue from the female role has come up time and again throughout this book. There is the "manic" rescue and the romantic rescue, for example. One of the most power-ful rescues remains the creative rescue, which for many women enables them to transcend their reality and enter into other states of being. Creativity is, in fact, meditative for these reasons. Through their creativity, women have managed to escape their roles and stave off depressions which often plague creative women in particular. Creative rescues come in all forms, as Renée reveals. Although her job is creative, she requires a different form of rescue:

> I work as an art director for film and television, and have spent all of my "thrill budget" on my horse, Nancy. I live for my moments with Nancy. I work 10-hour days, and then drive about 45 minutes outside the city to ride Nancy every night. This is a huge expense for me, but something that, I have to say, keeps me sane. In fact, when I chose to have Nancy and delay doing "grown-up things" like get a house,

I was worried that my husband wouldn't understand, but he does, and supports my relationship with Nancy, even though some of our friends wonder about me.

When I ride Nancy, I'm brought into another state of being. Because horses are so sensitive to our moods, you have to make absolutely sure that you are calm and centred before you ride, or else you risk being kicked or tossed in a ditch somewhere. My husband noticed something that I didn't: almost all of the people who are boarding a horse at my stable are women. I think that's very revealing about what women need in our culture.

Returning to the life of Eleanor Roosevelt, we can see how intellectual pursuits and activity are also forms of creative rescue. After learning of her husband's first affair, Eleanor realized that being a devoted wife and mother was not enough for her. After her grandmother's death, she commented to friends that her grandmother could have been a painter, "so much more." It was apparently at that point that Eleanor was resolved to do everything possible with her life. At 36, she joined the League of Women Voters, the Women's City Club and began to take courses. (Clearly, she was also entering a ripening.)

When she went to the White House as first lady, her boredom with the role is evident in these words from a letter: "I want to weep. My mind goes round and round like a squirrel in a cage. I want to run and I can't, and I despise myself." To combat the boredom, she became the most active first lady in history. She travelled, lectured, visited country after country as an ambassador and inspired millions. Yet, it is clear that her ceaseless activity was a rescue from her role, her unsatisfactory marriage and her bouts with depression.

We see a similar pattern in the former Princess Diana's life, who immersed herself in charity work to stave off boredom and depression. There is debate over whether Diana's causes were labours of love or creative rescue from the terribly confining role of a figurehead trapped in a loveless marriage. Shortly before her death in 1997, Diana, 36, was in full bloom amidst her own ripening and self-reinvention; she told the world in an interview that she wanted to be Britain's "ambassador of love."

Creativity also rescued the former Duchess of York, Sarah Ferguson, who pays her bills with Weight Watchers ads, but feeds her soul with the children's books she writes. (And as for the sexual wanderings of both Diana and Sarah into the arms of questionable liaisons, they were obviously looking for passion anywhere they could find it; clearly for them, passion was not lurking in Buckingham Palace.)

Ali MacGraw used her creativity to emerge from great depths of despair. After she gave up her acting career for Steve McQueen, and found herself alone again at 40 with no money, she immersed herself in yoga and put together a best-selling instructional yoga video. A former model, she also returned to her love for fashion and now produces a line of delicate handbags and shawls, beautifully hand-embroidered in India. In an interview with Jeanne Beker, MacGraw's appreciation of the art is apparent:

> The people making these are bringing ancient expertise. The embroidery is a traditional East Indian Muslim men's art. There's an unbelievable level of detail. That, for me, is

the magic. Somebody's in that work. It's not like we're cranking out 600,000 bags... But like most grown-ups I know, there's got to be time [for self-discovery]. While the fashion thing is fun, it isn't the cure for world starvation. Let's separate the urgency of whether this shawl is bought or not. I think there's real urgent stuff to do, like giving back to society to try and make it better for everybody. That is urgent work. And this [fashion business] is a lot of work, and it's fun, and it makes me happy, but if it doesn't work out I understand that I got on the wrong train.

Like the "horse lady," MacGraw, too, finds meditative rescue in her time with animals. She commented to Beker:

[Opportunities] are everywhere. And some of them aren't big deals. I think that's important, because in our society, we're always looking for the big deal, the big stock tip, the big whatever. But the little deals are where it's at for me. They're the sublime part of being alive. Little tiny things. At the end of every day where I live in New Mexico, I have to walk my dogs. And I do it as a meditation, just by myself, quietly. And just to observe every little thing as you go along is a miracle. And it sort of puts everything in perspective.

Quilting is a particularly well-known creative rescue. In African-American history, each quilted square represents a story or event in the life of the quilt-maker. Storytelling through quilting is used in an infinite variety of cultures, and was also used to tell the life story of people who died from

AIDS, as well as bring together the fragmented lives of loved ones who lost people to AIDS in the late 1980s, when AIDS funding was minimal.

Women and causes

The number of women who throw themselves into volunteer work is staggering. It amounts to millions of woman-hours. These causes are creative rescues, and are also one reason why women become possessive about their responsibilities within many of these organizations.

In my own experience with non-profit health organizations, I have encountered hundreds of women who tirelessly devote their bodies and souls to the cause. But when you ask them about their personal lives, it turns out that they usually lead very mundane, passionless existences. It's a pattern I've come to recognize. Some of the most devoted women do not even have the disease they are raising funds for, nor in fact, know anyone with that disease. There is even the term "professional volunteer" that describes the incredible, energetic, tireless fundraiser who can talk anyone into giving her organization a buck. I've seen these women in action, and I am amazed at their passion and dedication to causes that range from saving elephants from poachers, to raising support for rare diseases nobody ever heard of.

Women also become heavily involved in political or environmental causes as a means of creative rescue. Using their skills and intellect, they devote themselves to causes that offer them a place to put their talents. These causes also offer other fringe benefits, such as travel, if the organization is national and holds an annual general meeting (AGM).

Another pattern I've observed is that many women invite stormy encounters and passionate exchanges through the inter-personal dynamics that develop, as Sonia unwillingly noticed:

> At last year's AGM, the argument over who would remain as treasurer became so heated and divided, two women from opposite ends of the room got up and started scream-ing at each other—at the top of their lungs. Then they both burst into tears, and one left the room. It was so childish and embarrassing, and it all happened right in front of our medical advisory board. Our medical advisor stood up and actually had to stop the fight, and appealed to the organi-zation to rise above "these sort of outbursts" if they expected to keep their funding. I was mortified, and ashamed to be a member; I don't understand these women. Why do they let their petty emotions interfere with what we're all here for: to raise awareness.

Martha Stewart... and passion?

Why is Martha Stewart so successful? Because she offers creative rescue for millions of women through her lifestyle arts. She is essentially the mountain that comes to Mohammed. When women can't escape their roles, or choose them willingly, Martha offers some "good things" that help change their days and routine. And when it's called *Martha Stewart Living*, there is the invitation to come back to life and feel the small things (which she'll tell you is a good thing), even if it's just to wake up and smell fresh coffee... *sorbet.* Whether it's beautiful flowers, crafts or the hundreds of small things that take hours to make, she offers thousands of creative rescues every day through her program, magazine and Web site. Vera says of Martha:

> Don't insult Martha. I like her. I know she's too perfect, and nobody can live up to the Martha life without a staff of 50, but she allows us to dream about making life a little prettier. It's like escaping for a while. And I've made some of her things, and they've turned out really well. And yeah—it *can* take hours to make some of her things, but so what? Nobody watches Martha because she's real; we know it's an illusion, but we want to pretend that the role "works," even though we know it can suck!

MALE CONTROL OVER FEMALE CREATIVITY

In the 1986 film *Children of a Lesser God*, William Hurt, who plays a very creative teacher of deaf children, and deaf actress Marlee Matlin, who plays his lover, struggle over her "voice." She prefers to communicate through sign language; he wants to teach her to speak. He insists that he is a good teacher, and can teach her to speak well enough. She refuses, and in a poignant scene, articulates with her hands that until he can truly understand her, they will never have "the ultimate connection"—a term she communicates using a beautiful gesture that has meaning only in sign language.

She tells Hurt that "nobody can come inside my silence." This statement infuriates him. Her silence is, of course, the source of her power and passions. Hurt realizes that she can feel more of her life through her silence than hearing women. For example, she is able to flawlessly imitate the sound of ocean waves with her body using only motion and no sound. Hurt cannot accept that she has domain over how she chooses to use her voice, which drives her away from him. Directed by a woman, the struggle depicted in the film is a metaphor for all women, whose voices are continuously being controlled by the men in their lives.

In Canada, we can see this relationship in the career of Celine Dion, who does not appear to resent being "created" by her husband, René Angélil, to whom she is devoted. However, it is a well-known fact that he controls all facets of her career—which is her voice. This Eliza Doolittle/Henry Higgins battle of the man wanting to "create" the woman is classic. In fact, the more creative the woman, the more power-ful the struggle for control can become. Tina Turner struggled to regain control from her abusive husband, Ike. Cher felt she had lost control of her creativity to the late Sonny Bono when she left Sonny and Cher; Joe DiMaggio and Marilyn Monroe fought bitterly because he wanted her to give up her career at the height of her success (their marriage lasted for only 272 days). Then, when Monroe married playwright Arthur Miller, he tried to make her into a more serious actress than many feel she was capable of being (which drove her into deeper self-loathing and depressions), failing to acknowledge that she was already successful as a comedic actress. Debbie Reynolds lost all of her money—twice—to men who gambled away her hard-earned dollars. Mia Farrow's career was constantly controlled by her men, who ranged from Frank Sinatra to Woody Allen. (In fact, many observe how uncannily Allen's leading ladies begin to sound like one another.) Examples of this timeless struggle are legion.

What is it about men and control of women's creativity? Part of it has to do with the unconscious choices women make when they gravitate towards controlling men. Canadian writer Gwendolyn MacKewen, provides us with a good example of what frequently goes on. MacKewen was a good friend of Margaret Atwood's, part of a small circle of Canada's burgeoning literary scene, and a very successful poet in her own right. MacKewen was described as a beautiful, delicate young woman; yet she married what many call a Quasimodo figure—Canadian writer Milton Acorn, who was not only unattractive, but to some, even repulsive. MacKewen chose him, it is presumed, for her mind. MacKewen defended her choice, and said she loved Milton as an artist; she loved his strength and honesty. She was warned prior to marrying him, however, that he was mentally unstable. MacKewen was attracted to the role of nurturing the artist, for she was one herself. Her marriage to him interfered with the nurturing of her own art. In fact, the pattern of young creative women attaching themselves to chaotic males before they have fully established their own talent is common, and takes us into some of the themes discussed in chapter 5. MacKewen died of alcohol poisoning, but some rumour it was suicide.

This isn't always the pattern, of course. Margaret Atwood thought much more carefully about romantic involvement to protect her art. She says:

> Many people thought I was really quite cold and perhaps I am in a very specific way... I felt that if I was going to marry or form a permanent relationship then that individual had to know, from the beginning, who I was and what I was doing. I wasn't going to conceal it... (Sullivan, *The Red Shoes*: 157–58)

Atwood also comments on how creative women were perceived by men in her day:

> Creativity in those days was seen as ejaculatory... It goes with action painting. Jackson Pollock—what is that stuff on the canvas? We know! It was supposed to be a kind of spasm, instant painting, a kind of spasm of creation. And the poets adopted that as what a poem should be. It was essentially wanking off, whereas earlier poets, such as John Milton, were giving surrogate birth. 'O Muse, descend, impregnate me. I will bear this book within me; then I'll give birth to it.' The earlier metaphor was very much an appropriation of female birth giving, and they then used that as the reason women couldn't write: because they could have the real thing. Whereas in the fifties ejaculatory school, women couldn't write because they couldn't jerk off and cause dribbles on the page. (Sullivan, *The Red Shoes*: 104).

For the countless unknown artists among us, our art is often forsaken to please our men, as Louise reveals:

> Before I got married, my husband fully supported my painting and sculpture. But after a couple of years, he started to complain about the mess I would make in our apartment. So I cut down on my work, and eventually stopped altogether. I get angry when my husband innocently asks me in front of friends (when we're out in a group—always in a group!), "Yeah, Louise, why did you ever stop painting…? You were so talented."

Gwen shares this tale of cruelty and abuse, which was wound around her creativity:

> When I got married at 20, I was actually a trained concert pianist. My ex-husband was a controlling SOB who was an academic (my mother forced me to marry him because she thought he was going places that I couldn't). He was always monopolizing conversations and trying to be the centre of attention. You know that type—the "expert" in everything…?
>
> At parties, people would ask me to play, and I could see on his face that he couldn't stand the praise and attention I would get. I wanted to send our daughter for piano lessons. He said he didn't want her to take piano lessons because he "didn't want her to be like me." In truth, he wasn't bad for an amateur, and he *was* able, with absolutely no training, to play. People who aren't musicians couldn't tell that

he was pounding when he shouldn't, though. My ear was trained, and listening to him squeak through Mozart was sometimes more than I could bear. But I said nothing. *Always* I was silent.

One day, I was playing Bach. He told me I was too fat to sit on the bench, and that it would break; he also said he didn't want me to play that "goddamned church music" and forbid me to even listen to Bach and threatened to smash all my records. Essentially, he made it impossible for me to play. I stopped playing. A part of me was dead anyway. He sold our piano without asking me, and then after he threw me out of the house, bought an expensive grand piano for himself.

Ultimately, women have much more creative control, and the freedom to create, than they once did. But when our feelings of low self-worth become reinforced by life experiences, we may doubt our creativity when it is questioned. Or, we may give it up too willingly in order to get love or approval. Valerie Gibson, commented to me in an interview: "All my life I've worked very passionately for men's dreams." Only in recent years has Gibson begun to work passionately for her own. But she observes that men who aren't passionate are usually attracted to those who are. "The problem is, they want to control it, smush it."

The power to create, and the creative ways we have to empower ourselves—in all the various forms—comes from our sense of mortality. We all want to leave a piece of ourselves behind; or at least, live more creatively while we're here. We all know our final destination, too, and everything we do in our lives is preparation for the next stage. Valerie Gibson says: "The pathway to death is the best route of all of them—so interesting and full." She is, of course, talking about living. We spend our lives, whether we want to admit it or not, looking for meaning in our passionate acts—sex and death. The two acts, as you'll see in the next chapter, are a lot more similar than you think.

8

ACTS OF PASSION
SEX AND DEATH

There are two experiences that drive us forward, propel us into living life to its fullest: sex and death. These two experiences mirror one another. When we have sex, we actually simulate the dying experience in many ways. Research into death and dying has shown that the dying experience, while full of pain and suffering, can also lead to an exalted state. It is a passage into another realm of being that a lot of us have visited before many times—each time we sexually climax. The heights of pain and the heights of pleasure meet at the same station so to speak. All of the religious and romantic motifs surrounding sex and death link them as well, as they are the two acts that bridge our life cycle. The star-crossed lovers trying to reach death together is a recurring theme in *Romeo and Juliet, Wuthering Heights*, and hundreds of romantic works. Wedding vows are even sealed with "till death do us part." This chapter looks more closely at the two acts of passion that drive all living beings forward. In a nutshell: we *live* for our deaths.

THE LITTLE DEATH (LE PETIT MORT)

When it comes to passion, the French seem to know what they're talking about. So when I first learned that the French phrase for orgasm was "little death" or "petit mort" I felt that my theory about sex and death was validated. If you look at the healthy sexual experience—meaning, mutually satisfactory sex between two consenting adults—you realize that it has a life of its own. There is a steady progression towards a climactic event, where we enter an "altered state" and where our bodies and minds become one with another's. Then we fall into a deep sleep, and we feel slightly reborn for a while. We love that altered state so much, we spend half our lives in pursuit of the experience over and over and over again.

The healthy sexual experience can help us prepare for the dying experience, as we learn to surrender our vulnerability, and learn to trust our bodies to take us to that altered state. But what happens when we are denied a good sexual experience? When we never learn to surrender our bodies completely, we begin to fear that surrender as we age. Fearing the surrender can make for a more difficult dying experience—an experience that we all have to face one day whether we like it or not.

When it's not as good for her as it is for him

Gloria Steinem notes that women will often miss their own sexual experience and become simply a "pleasurer" for their partner's body; or worse, they completely suppress their sexual experiences and live vicariously through the experiences of their partners. For a lot of women, in fact, orgasm is a foreign experience that they have never known. For many women, the sexual act is also fragmented into parts without a whole, as Marjorie shares:

> I am known for my blow jobs. I am an amazing magician in this department, and still get calls from ex-lovers telling me they miss that, and cannot find another woman who was willing to do for them what I did. But the pleasure for me in giving a blow job is only the control I have over the man's pleasure. I like being in control; the blow job does nothing for me sexually at all. In fact, my two secrets to an amazing blow job (it's okay—you can publish this recipe) is to loosen your tension in the jaw completely (this takes a lot of practice) and to make sure you squeeze the balls with each forward thrust, while simultaneously stroking the shaft. Men also go crazy if you suck on one ball—as though you're inhaling it. It's easier to demonstrate it... you don't have an anatomically correct Ken doll on you by any chance...? I think my teeth are perfectly proportioned, too, so maybe that has something to do with the mouth action I get so many compliments on! [*Note*: Marjorie is telling us how sex for her is an experience of technical expertise rather than pleasure.]

Ruby's sexual experiences were wound around the moods of her partner:

I was the textbook dancer, recovering, like most dancers, from an eating disorder that lasted for a good 10 years. I'm now in my mid-30s, and have come to realize that I substitute men for food to avoid dealing with my own intense emotions that have plagued me all my life. I have always gravitated towards very sexual relationships with volatile men, and the sexual experience is always a crapshoot. If my boyfriend feels good, and the experience is good for him, I'm happy. If my boyfriend does not feel satisfied, neither do I. I spend so much time reading these men, that I am often exhausted, and just don't feel energized enough to worry about my own sexual pleasure. When I read men well and respond appropriately to their sexual needs, my stock goes up with the man, and I am more valuable to him. I guess somewhere inside I know that if my so-called stock loses value for the man, I'm going to have to build it back up all by myself. I just don't think I can commit to that. Learning to be true to my body's physical needs—learning to eat again—was hard enough. But having to learn to pleasure my body seems an impossible task right now.

In her book *The Vagina Monologues*, award-winning poet and playwright Eve Ensler simply began interviewing women about their vaginas, and uncovered many deeply wounded women whose sexual experiences were either never fully realized, or were, in fact, memories of such torture and pain, they avoided sexuality in their adult lives. One particularly disturbing excerpt reads (Ensler notes that we are to read this with a Jewish Queens accent):

Down there? I haven't been down there since 1953... There was this boy, Andy Leftkov. He was cute—well, I thought so... He asked me out for a date in his car... I remember thinking that my legs were too long for the seat. I have long legs. They were bumping up against the dashboard. I was looking at my big kneecaps when he just kissed me in this surprisingly "take me by control like they do in the movies" kind of way. And I got excited, so excited, and, well, there was a flood down there. I couldn't control it. It was like this force of passion, this river of life just flooded out of me, right through my panties, right onto the car seat of his new white Chevy BelAir. It wasn't pee and it was smelly—well, frankly, I didn't really smell anything at all, but he said, Andy said, that it smelled like sour milk and it was staining his car seat. I was "a stinky weird girl," he said. I wanted to explain that his kiss had caught me off guard, that I wasn't normally like this. I tried to wipe the flood up with my dress. It was a new yellow primrose dress and it looked so ugly with the flood on it. Andy drove me home and he never, never said another word and when I got out and closed his car door, I closed the whole store. Locked it. Never opened for business again. I dated some after that, but the idea of flooding made me too nervous. I never even got close again. (Ensler: 25–28)

The sad truth is that many women do not experience sexual pleasure at all, and until the twentieth century, were not even aware that they ought to. Historically, the word "vagina" comes from the Latin word for "sheath" (as in a sheath for the penis). It was once thought that its sole function was for male arousal. The lubrication was thought to be solely for the man's enjoyment. I would be remiss, too, not to mention the millions of women who have undergone female circumcision, also known as female genital mutilation, in which the clitoris is removed completely, and for some, most of the vulva. This is something I discuss at great length in *The Gynecological Sourcebook*, but in the context of women and passion, it is a cultural surgery that robs women of feeling their lives so much to the core, it is heartbreaking to ponder.

Women will also trade sexual pleasure for being hugged and held. One of the most revealing surveys of women's sexual attitudes was conducted in 1985 through an Ann Landers column. Landers asked her readers: "Would you be content to be held close and treated tenderly and forget about the act?" Seventy-two percent of the 90,000 women surveyed said yes. Of those 72 percent, 40 percent were under 40 years of age.

One of the most significant barriers to women's sexual pleasure is their body image. Women who feel unattractive often can't enjoy sex. In one study of attractiveness and sexuality, all participants said they felt sexier and more easily aroused when they believed they were attractive. This suggests that women think they must look sexy before they can feel sexy, which plays into many of the complex eating behaviours discussed in chapter 6. On a more ridiculous note, 1970s sex researcher Seymour Fisher actually conducted a study to figure out whether women in sexy dresses had more orgasms. His findings were inconclusive.

What Gloria Steinem feels is at the core of the "appearance versus sexuality" debate is that women are afraid to "look funny" during the act of sex. They are afraid to openly enjoy themselves, utter sounds and break out of the polite, ladylike mode of being, as Virginia reveals:

> I taught myself to silently orgasm when I was a teenager. I would never "go all the way" with my boyfriends, but I would allow them to finger me. I would orgasm silently, and then get very ticklish. I would tell them to stop, and interrupted the session by saying I wanted to go home. Perplexed, the poor boy I would do this to (there were many!) would wonder what he did wrong. Why did I *suddenly* want to stop? I wanted to stop before he realized that I came. I was too embarrassed to admit that I came. It took me years to learn how to make sound. I'm sure many cases of blue balls had my name on it.

Naomi Wolf, author of *The Beauty Myth*, asserts that the woman's naked body has become so distorted through pornography and other imagery, that it looks inhuman, "perfected beyond familiarity." The result is that the normal body is perceived by women to look more abnormal than the abnormal beauty standards. Pornography also distorts the normal sexual experience into the abnormal. Says Wolf:

> So rare is it to see sexual explicitness in the context of love and intimacy on screen that it seems our culture treats tender sexuality as if it were deviant or depraved, while embracing violent or degrading sex as right and healthy. (Wolf: 140)

Pornography falls into the realm of unhealthy passions, where men are looking for the quick fix. However, because their appearance is so tied into their desirability and sexual pleasure, women can become addicted to "men's eyes"—how they appear to look, rather than how they feel.

ALL ABOUT EVE

Sex researcher Alfred Kinsey believed that religious beliefs were powerful barriers to women's experiences. Allowing ourselves to surrender to the sexual experience means, for many, to surrender our guilt about sex. The great drama of human sin begins with Adam and Eve in the Garden of Eden. Though some speculate that there was sexual activity in paradise, most agree that there was no sex at all in Eden because there was no death in Eden. It's not until Adam and Eve eat from the tree of knowledge that they discover their own sexuality; they also discover at the same time that they will die. This is Original Sin.

Many theologians insist, however, that the sin is not the sex, but the arrogance of disobeying God. For the sin of arrogance, or self-awareness about their mortality, Adam and Eve are expelled from Eden, and from this point on, they will know both passion and death. For her role as temptress, in which she is blamed for our fall from grace, Eve is punished; God tells her that he will greatly increase her pains in childbearing: "In pain, you shall bring forth children, yet your desire shall be for your husband and he shall rule over you." (Genesis 3:16)

Sexual passion, therefore, becomes synonymous with pain, and for many women, death, as frequently women died giving birth. The message of the story of Eve is that women invite death when they surrender to their desires. Jungian analyst Marion Woodman interprets Eve offering Adam the apple as offering man consciousness, and in a sense giving birth to man.

The passion of childbirth

The twisted moral dilemma of giving birth is that, although it is what leads to our consciousness, it also leads to the painful realization that we will die. But is death also a birth? A rabbi who deals with death-and-dying issues told me this tale of two twins in the womb, about to be born. One twin cries: "I can't believe it; it's over. We're dying. Life was so short." The other twin eagerly awaits the passage and says: "What do you mean? Life is just beginning." The point is that whether birth is the passage into death, or death the passage into birth, sexuality is the bridge.

The German philosopher Georg Friedrich Hegel said:

> The birth of children is the death of parents... the child is the very being of their love which is external to them [and, inversely, the child will attain his own being] in separating from its source, a separation in which that source finds its end." (de Beauvoir, *The Second Sex*: 497)

One author puts it more ominously—the mother dooms her child to death in giving it life. But this concept also tells us more about how men perceive their mothers and lovers:

> Thus what man cherishes and detests first of all in woman— loved one or mother—is the fixed image of his animal

destiny; it is the life that is necessary to his existence but that condemns him to the finite and to death. From the day of his birth man begins to die: this is the truth incarnated in the Mother. In procreation he speaks for the species against himself: he learns this in his wife's embrace; in excitement and pleasure, even before he has engendered, he forgets his unique ego. Although he endeavors to distinguish mother and wife, he gets from both a witness to one thing only: his mortal state. He wishes to venerate his mother and love his mistress; at the same time he rebels against them in disgust and fear." (de Beauvoir, *The Second Sex*: 165, 166)

These sentiments are reinforced in religious artwork, such as in Hans Baldung's *Eve, the Serpent, and Death*, in which Adam isn't even present in Eden. In this sixteenth-century painting, Eve's body is presented frontally, exposed to the viewer, and she clutches the apple in her right hand. But Death grips her left arm with his left hand, literally attaching Eve to death—hence, sexual desire to death.

THE BIG DEATH

It is my "wild" theory that somehow the "little death" is preparation for the big one. If we can surrender to the little death, perhaps we can unconsciously prepare ourselves for surrender to the big one. Everybody dies, of course. But few of us are around to witness death unless we work in the clinical health care setting. Most people have only one or two experiences in their lifetime of being with someone who is dying. In my own life, I've seen four people less than 24 hours prior to their passing. Let me share what I've seen:

In the first case, a 38-year-old friend was dying of melanoma, and although she was blind, she thought she could still see, and behaved as though she was seeing me. We held hands, and it was terribly important for her to tell me how much she loved her mother. In the second case, my grandfather was dying from end-stage esophageal cancer. We held hands, and it was terribly important for him to tell me that he loved me, and it was difficult (but I did it) for me to tell him that I loved him. In the third case, my 89-year-old aunt was dying of a blood disorder. We held hands, and it was terribly important for her to know whether I believed in the afterlife. I told her I did, and that her dead husband would help bring her over to the other side. It was what she needed to hear to die; an hour later she was dead. And in the fourth case, I saw my 36-year-old best friend's husband. He was dying of end-stage esophageal cancer. We held hands. He was very sweaty, and commented that my hand was "nice and cool." It was terribly important for him to say to me and my partner (a friend of his with whom I was having a stormy romance): "I love you guys; life is short, so if you can find any kind of happiness together, go for it."

I find it odd how similar these four experiences were. The overwhelming common factor was the dying's urgent need to communicate something while holding my hands. Without going into detail about the symptoms of various illnesses, in a very general way, when we are dying, the physical manifestations of death mirror the sexual: we become short of breath; we sweat profusely; we are at our most vulnerable emotionally and physically, and may reach out to touch a loved one's hand or feel a great need to clutch it; we moan (in pain); we spasm; we leak fluids; we can go in and out of the conscious state; some bodies can also "flap" around; and most of all, if we are conscious, we feel consumed with love.

According to my girlfriend, her husband kept repeating "I love you" for the last week of his life to everyone he saw. When we are dying we are at our most forgiving; few people die unwilling to forgive the sins of the living, even though they may not have an opportunity to say "I forgive you." And few people die unwilling to say "I'm sorry" for the sins they've committed during their lifetime, even though they may not have the opportunity to say so.

Palliative care specialists repeatedly caution health care practitioners not to interfere with closure. The point of palliative care is to relieve pain so the dying can have closure with the living, and feel their lives instead of pain.

What I'm describing is the normal dying experience, which unfortunately can become corrupted and interfered with through medical technology. To be robbed of our most passionate moments, however, probably has consequences for our death experiences. Health care practitioners are starting to be concerned about the notion of prolonging death, which has led to policy changes around what are called heroic measures (reviving the dead) in people whose deaths are imminent. Feeding tubes, breathing support and other devices can be used to make people at the end of life die more comfortable deaths. But they can also prolong death, or interfere with it, which ultimately can rob us of this moment.

Brenda, who has spent her life in the clinical setting caring for the dying, shares this:

> A lot of people in health care find caring for the dying a burden, which is astounding to me. They don't realize that our role is to bear witness to the most important time in someone's life. We are privileged to witness someone's death. When I am around the families of the dying, and my dying patients, the power differentials between "doctor," "nurse" or "patient" disappear. We are all midwives to the death experience, and I for one am transformed by witnessing such experiences. I'm trying to write about this in some way, and would like to get across to my colleagues that they should step out of their clinical hierarchical roles and learn what they can from the dying. It's an opportunity for *us*. They'll die anyway whether we're around or not. We are powerless to stop the process, but we can learn from it.

Why we're obsessed with sex

Understanding the similarities between the "little death" and the "big death" helps explain why, in this culture, we are so obsessed with sex. The surrender to the flesh is a necessary experience for our spirits and souls—and it is an experience we're all going to have whether we want it or not. In other cultures, the lifeforce energy that emanates from the body is cultivated much more than it is in the West. Here, we essentially cut off the mind from the body, as we see in our system of alophathic medicine—which means we treat the body part rather than the whole body. Sex in Western culture becomes, for many, the only avenue we have to feel something— connection, life, flesh... which is why it is everywhere, and why, when you're looking for books on passion you'll usually find books about sex instead of feeling. (Try searching for passion in cyberspace and see what comes up!)

We have created a perverse set of rules and images around the sexual experience, at the expense of women's bodies. We, as humans, live for that surrender and connection to another human being. But for many, even admitting that this is what we are after feels not allowed, and as a culture, we have invented perverse ways to rob ourselves of the total sexual experience. Sam Keen, author of *The Passionate Life*, believes that the sado-masochistic practices around the sexual experience are about making one another the sexual object rather than the subject so we can have sex "safely" without the feeling and the connection.

A PASSIONATE LIFE

I wanted to end this book by exploring one of the most passionate lives I could find in a well-known woman, so you could relate to her, too. I think you'll agree that I chose well. It is Elizabeth Taylor. Her best-selling perfume is even called Passion. By looking at this woman's life, we can see not only how the sexual and death experiences merge, but also how all of the chapters in this book come together through her choices and experiences.

Most people know Elizabeth Taylor for her great beauty (she is known as, arguably, the most beautiful woman in the world), many relationships and marriages. But few people realize how many times she's faced critical illness and that she was near death more than once. This is what many feel has fuelled her unshakeable passion for life. It's interesting, too, to note the number of times she's bounced between the "wild man" and the "stable man," and the number of times she's left one man for another, without much time alone until her later years. You can find just about everything you need to know about women and passion by examining her life. Biographers marvel, too, at how her body would completely change, depending upon whom she was with. One psychologist noted that women have a "shape-shifting ability" of conforming to others' expectations, which is more true in Taylor's case than perhaps any other public woman's. One biographer writes of Taylor's relationships:

> She has known—been married to, had affairs with, been mixed up with—some of the weirdest, most abusive, addictive, profligate, polymorphously perverse men imaginable—brutes, even... some of the marriages were melodramas; a few were tragedies... But Elizabeth Taylor, imagination made flesh, has lived out her desires, a series of overlapping lives with a cast of thousands. (*Talk Magazine*: 1:2, 1999)

First and foremost, Taylor was a child star (her first film was *National Velvet*) who felt trapped in her role—as most women. She always felt owned by the big Hollywood studio system and had very little freedom. (She noted in an interview that she and Michael Jackson's close friendship was founded on common child star traumas they both experienced.) So when you look at her personal life, remember that all the while, she was trying to break free as an individual, and may well have gone to crazy places for her passion. (We actually see a very similar life pattern with Judy Garland, also a child star, who also married many times, and struggled with weight issues and addictions; her life ended in a drug overdose in 1969.)

After Taylor's first marriage in 1950, at age 18, to hotel heir Nicky Hilton, Jr. (wild and too immature), she married Michael Wilding (older and very stable) in 1952, with whom she had two sons. She left Wilding in 1957 to marry producer Mike Todd (wild man, bordering on violent), with whom she had a daughter. She was madly in love with Todd, but in 1958, Todd was killed in a plane crash in New Mexico. Taylor became very depressed during her grieving period, and she turned to her friend Eddie Fisher (stable Mr. Nice Guy) during this time, who left his wife, actress Debbie Reynolds, for Taylor. It was a scandal at the time. But Taylor earned back public support when she almost died in 1961 from pneumonia. It was so touch and go, she received an emergency tracheotomy. She later said she won her first Oscar not for *Butterfield 8*, but for not dying of pneumonia. (She won her second Oscar for *Who's Afraid of Virginia Woolf* in 1966, a film which I discuss in chapter 6.)

Then she left Eddie for Richard Burton (1964 through 1976—wild, moody, terribly erratic and alcoholic), a highly sexual relationship, and a time I believe Taylor was in her ripening. When she met Burton on the set of *Cleopatra* in

1963, she had been paid an unheard-of salary of a million dollars, which she asked for as a joke that the studios took seriously. On the set, Taylor and Burton were visibly involved, which was complicated by Taylor's marriage to Fisher and Burton's marriage to Sybil Williams. They both divorced their respective spouses to marry each other. Taylor later called him "the great love of her life," and it was a stormy off-again/on-again romance (they divorced in 1974 and remarried in 1975, only to divorce again in 1976) that had manic overtones.

Taylor and Burton spent an enormous amount of money; Burton bought her a gargantuan diamond ring that became widely publicized *and* criticized. In an interview, Taylor said: "It was too much passion for either of us to bear."

Taylor and Burton were the first couple to be besieged by paparrazi, something we take for granted today. But in 1964, it was new for the media to be obsessed with a couple. The media, and the world, were obsessed with the passion of their relationship, of course. They became Liz and Dick to the world, and all of their fights, ups and downs, were recorded. (When Princess Diana was killed, Taylor, in an interview, described how terrifying it can be to be in a speeding car trying to run away from the press—a feeling she knew all too well.)

Taylor began to drink when she was with Burton, who was an alcoholic, and it was possible that the alcohol helped her to keep pace with the sharp-tongued Burton, frequently drunk himself. Burton said of Taylor: "Our love is so furious that we burn each other out."

After she and Burton finally ended their marriage, she boomeranged into security again when she married John Warner (stable but quite dull), a U.S. Republican senator from

Virginia. Taylor tried to be a Washington wife, but she became very unhappy. At this point, Taylor gained an enormous amount of weight, substituting food for what I believe was her lost passion with Burton. Burton passed away in 1984 from an alcohol-related fall that resulted in a brain hemorrhage. Taylor and Warner divorced in 1982, and a year later, Taylor entered the Betty Ford Clinic for treatment for her alcoholism.

Throughout Taylor's life, she also suffered repeatedly from lower-back problems and chronic pain, and became addicted to painkillers, entering Betty Ford again in 1988. It was here she met her last husband, Larry Fortensky, a construction worker 30 years younger than Taylor, whom she married in 1991. Fortensky was an odd choice in that he came from a blue-collar background, but it tells us something about Taylor's need for connection. They met in the same recovery program, and Taylor said in interviews that they actually had a lot in common in their struggles with addiction. Ultimately, Fortensky and Taylor were a mismatch and divorced in 1997.

From the mid-1990s on, Taylor experienced a series of life-threatening health problems: she had hip replacements in 1994 and 1995, as well as a benign brain tumour removed in 1997. In 1998 and 1999, she suffered two serious falls in her home, injuring her lower back again. She has, in fact, been struggling with chronic pain since her brush with near death in the early 1960s.

Because she's endured so much suffering in her own life, she has the ability to "co-suffer"—to be compassionate. Taylor co-founded the American Foundation for AIDS Research (AmFAR) after her good friend Rock Hudson died of AIDS in 1985 (they met on the set of *Giant* in 1956, and had been close ever since; Taylor had also been close to Montgomery Cliff, who was a bisexual, whom she met on the set of *Raintree County* in 1957). Her daughter-in-law also contracted AIDS through a blood transfusion during childbirth. (One of the best books I've used for my research on women and AIDS is one that was quietly published by E. Taylor Publishing. Hmmm... wonder who *that* could be!) Taylor was the first Hollywood name to support AIDS, which shows her courage as an "outside the box" thinker. By 1999, she had raised an estimated $50 million for AIDS research. Her perfumes—Passion and White Diamonds—bring in an estimated $200 million annually, much of which she donates. In 1999, Taylor was made a dame of the British Empire by Queen Elizabeth II.

As an artist, Taylor has used her creativity to its fullest. As an actor, her ability to portray the tortured passions of women comes through in roles such as Maggie the Cat, in *Cat on a Hot Tin Roof*, and Martha, in *Who's Afraid of Virginia Woolf.* But she reinvented herself long before it was popular through launching perfume and using her celebrity for a cause. Countless female Hollywood actors have copied her, but no one can touch her. One of her biographers summed up her life, and perhaps this book, best:

> For all she's put into these doomed relationships, she's always managed to get out—and to find freedom and joy through the creative process of acting... Elizabeth has an appetite for life, and appetite was the word that kept occurring to me when I thought of her. It was zest, and also a hunger, which was somehow never satisfied. In this hunger she is at her most Elizabethan... her feet are squarely on the ground, she is literal-minded, and her appetite is literally that, a desire to devour. (*Talk Magazine*: 1:2, 1999)

Passionate women feel their lives by surviving, reinventing themselves and not being afraid of living. Interestingly, both Valerie Gibson and Jeanne Beker, both extremely passionate women, tell me they are survivors, and made the same comment to me about how they see life: Gibson referred to life as a sandbox in which we have to play: "Life is messy; we have to get messy, and play in that sand." Beker referred to life as a diving board and said that we "just have to get in that water regardless of whether it's freezing or muddy or rocky."

Gibson, now 60, has definitely played in the sandbox. Her life includes five marriages, raising a mentally challenged daughter, rebuilding her life from nothing at age 45 (after walking away from a marriage) and a wild variety of interim jobs throughout her mainstay career as a journalist. These interim jobs included interior design, real estate and astrology, but Gibson was also Britain's first female professional scuba diver. Most of us know Gibson as the former *Toronto Sun* fashion editor, and currently, the *Toronto Sun* sex/relationship columnist. She insists that for her, life is about "exploring the boundaries."

Beker, 48, who has interviewed the most interesting and beautiful women in the world, says that the passionate woman is untamed. She grows like a wildflower. She can't be coiffed or gardened or controlled. The daughter of Holocaust survivors, Beker insists that her parents instilled a sense of liberty and freedom into her, enabling her to not be afraid to try things and fail. As she ages, she realizes that "everything we do is training and preparation for something else." Of her own life, she says: "I've lived the life I wanted to live; no regrets. At the end of the day, if I can say that I've been true to myself—

brutally honest with myself—that's all I care about. The older we become the more *ourselves* we become."

My parting thoughts to you about women and passion is this: no woman has this "passion thing" all worked out. If you're reflecting on your life, and thinking only about the mistakes you've made, or your regrets, don't do that to yourself. That's what life is for. We're here to try things on and check things out—to feel our bodies and mortality. Albert Einstein said that the person who's never made a mistake has never lived. So embrace your choices and understand them. You can choose something else tomorrow. Above all, don't be afraid to *live*. As Valerie Gibson says in the foreword to this book: There is no life without passion.

PUBLISHER'S NOTE: Roughly 75 sources were used for this book. Due to space restrictions, we were unable to provide a bibliography. This data can be accessed at **www.SaraHealth.com** or through the publisher.

"I hope that *Women & Passion* will encourage women to unleash their fettered feelings and discover that without passion in life, there is no life."
— VALERIE GIBSON, SEX AND RELATIONSHIP COLUMNIST AND AUTHOR OF
AN OLDER WOMAN'S GUIDE TO YOUNGER MEN

What are the consequences to women who suppress their passion—or who indulge in it? And how can women rekindle and harness passion for a healthier and more satisfying life?

In chapters such as The Ripening, Consuming Passions, Unhealthy Passions and Creative Passions, and through research on women as varied as Jane Goodall, Elizabeth Taylor and Margaret Atwood, author Sara Rosenthal explores the roots, fruits and consequences of passion lost, passion denied and passion regained.

Readers of *Women & Passion* will recognize aspects of their own patterns and behaviours in the universal cycles of passion. And they'll discover not only how they got where they are, but how to move on to a fuller and richer stage in their lives.

M. Sara Rosenthal is the author of more than 15 widely recommended health books. Her work is reviewed and reprinted on over 500 Web sites and she is a frequent contributor to WebMD, the largest health Web site to date.

An Associate of the University of Toronto Centre for Health Promotion—a World Health Organization Collaborating Centre—Rosenthal has her Masters degree in Sociology and Bioethics from the University of Toronto's Joint Centre for Bioethics, where she is now completing her Ph.D.

For more information, visit www.sarahealth.com.

$24.95

Prentice
Hall
Canada

A Pearson Company

ISBN 0-13-088404-9

0 57812 88404 5

ISBN 0-13-088404-9

9 780130 884046